# ADAM SMITH, MARX, KEYNES AND FRIEDMAN

## AN "INTERVIEW"

## Domingos de Gouveia Rodrigues

# Summary

# 1.Introduction

Economic thought has suffered, over the past centuries, remarkable progress and, despite the fact that the contemporary world is characterized by the existence of distressing problems in many regions of the planet, such as diseases, misery, hunger, unemployment, incomprehension among peoples leading to wars and the latent state of international tension and violence, understood in its broadest sense, undoubtedly all currents of economic thought, throughout history, from Greek and Roman philosophers, to the scholastics of the Middle Ages, to mercantilists (these not much clearly), by 18th century liberals, by 19th century socialists and more recently, in the 20th century, by John Maynard Keynes (1888-1946) and Milton Friedman (1912-2006), emphasize the need to seek a more just, free and balanced world where man can have access to growing social well-being, materialized in the continuous meeting of his socio-political-economic needs and in the development of his spirit.

The reasons for not fully achieving these goals - despite the remarkable scientific and technological progress achieved by Humanity - may lie in the nature of the human being himself, unequally endowed with aptitudes, desires and goals, an insatiable conqueror and increasingly self-centered.

However, this moral and philosophical stance of great thinkers gives encouragement to those who envision a better world and, although the recipes are different - throughout history there has been a huge diversity of ideas and systems, many of them totally antagonistic (some liberal, others centralizing) - the ultimate goal is always the good of humanity.

In this book, we present some ideas that we consider fundamental to understand the thinking of four great Men - Adam Smith (1723-1790), Karl Marx (1818-1883), John Maynard Keynes (1883-1946) and Milton Friedman (1912-2006). Sometimes in agreement, almost always divergent, their reading shows us how complex, different and grandiose human thought is and how to interpret the world around him.

Put in the form of an "interview", let us pretend that the issues raised here are being said by them today. Without a doubt, we will be surprised to see many of their ideas with remarkable relevance, although none of the four is still alive.

"Let's talk", then, to Adam Smith, Marx, Keynes and Friedman.

# 2. An "Interview" with Adam Smith (1723-1790)

"It stands to reason that the product of two days or two hours of work is worth twice as much as what normally only requires a day or an hour of work".

Adam Smith

# 2.1. Who Was Adam Smith (1723-1790)

Scottish economist Adam Smith was born in Kirkcaldy, Fifeshire, in 1723, and died in Edinburgh on July 17, 1790. A student of Francis Hutcheson (1694-1746), studied in Glasgow, transferring to Balliol College, Oxford in 1740. A friend of David Hume (1711-1776), he was appointed professor of logic at the University of Glasgow in 1751, switching his chair to moral philosophy in 1752. In 1759, Adam Smith published "Theory of Moral Sentiments", a book of great repercussion.

Smith's contact with the physiocrats, who formed a French school of economic thought, under the leadership of François Quesnay (1694-1774), stems from the fact that he abandoned teaching in 1763 to become the preceptor of the Duke of Bucclengh on a year and a half trip to France and Switzerland. Back in Kirkcaldy, in 1766, with the pension received from the duke, he dedicates himself intensively to his great work "An Inquiry Into the Nature and Cause of the Wealth of Nations", published in 1776, year of the independence of the United States. The success of this work was remarkable, with five editions still in Smith's life. In 1778 he was appointed customs inspector, a position like that of his father, who was a defending judge and customs intervener, ending his professional career as rector of the University of Glasgow, a position he has exercised since 1787.

Smith's ideas developed at a time when "Mercantilism" was the relevant economic thought, whose doctrines defended the assumption that a nation's wealth was determined, fundamentally, by foreign trade. In this sense, if the country exported more than it imported, it would cause a net inflow of currency (precious metals), a factor that for mercantilists determined the country's wealth. These doctrines greatly encouraged protectionism in favor of an increase in the trade balance.

Adam Smith, the father of political economics, laid the foundations for a new science that would influence not only the scholars of his day, but also all future generations.

Adam Smith's economic thinking reflects the historical moment of his time, characterized by the beginning of the Industrial Revolution and the unrestrained antagonism between the landowning nobility and the emerging manufacturing bourgeoisie who defended the economic freedom that would boost their investments.

The basis of this thought comes from Hutcheson's "natural" moralism, deism and empiricist idealism, mainly from David Hume, influencing Smith's formation, which establishes in "Theory of Moral Sentiments" the ethical program of the ideology of economic and social liberalism that will characterize the seminal work "The Wealth of Nations".

Unlike mercantilists (emphasis on the circulation of goods) and physiocrats (emphasis on the role of agriculture), Smith chooses Work as the central agent of economic theory, for him the basis of nations' wealth and the real measure of the exchange value of all goods.

Defender of economic liberalism, for Smith the force that would lead to the best economic organization, was literally opposed to mercantilism (which led to protectionism) and against state intervention in the economy.

Contrary to what many people think, Smith had a social vision, because for him "no society can flourish and be happy if most of its elements are poor and miserable".

Smith develops concepts, such as surplus value and exchange value, which will be taken up by Marx in his critical analysis of Capitalism, and formulates the classic principles of tax, constituting, still, the first analyst who starts with the use of scientific methods to describe the behavior of the economy. Smith's legacy transcends his time, constituting a masterful work that requires reflection by all those interested in discussing the role of economic liberalism in the construction of a free, just and pluralist society.

## 2.2. An "Interview" with Adam Smith

Q - Professor Smith, you have emphasized the importance of the division of labor as a factor in increasing productivity. How does this happen?

A - "The increasing development of labor productivity, and the increase in the commitment, dexterity and discernment to which it is linked, seems to have been caused by the division of labor. The effects of the division of labor on the general activity of society will be more easily understood if we consider the way it is carried out in some industries. It is generally assumed that the division of labor is more developed in less important activities; however, this does not mean that in larger industries the division of labor is not greater (...) On the contrary, in large factories designed to supply the needs of a greater number of people, each branch of activity involves a number of workers so high that it is impossible to keep them working in a single facility (...) To give an example, we can mention a very weak industry but whose division of labor has been very noticeable: the manufacture of pins (...) One man carries the wire, another straightens it, a third cuts it, a fourth sharpens the end, a fifth prepares the upper end to receive the head; (...) The important job of making pins is therefore divided into about eighteen different operations (...) I had the opportunity to see a small factory of this type, in which only ten men were employed (...) But, despite being very poor, and possessing only the machinery strictly necessary, they managed, when they struggled, to manufacture about twelve pounds of pins a day. Each pound corresponds to more than four thousand medium sized pins. These ten people, therefore, were able to produce more than forty-eight thousand pins a day. If we divide this work by the number of workers, we can consider that each one of them produces 4,800 pins a day; but if they worked separately from each other, and without being educated for this particular branch of production, they would not be able to produce twenty pins, or perhaps even a single pin a day."

Q - Professor Smith, what are the reasons for this extraordinary increase in productivity?

A - "This considerable increase in production, which, due to the division of labor, the same number of people is capable of carrying out, is due to three different circumstances: first, the increase in the skill of each worker; second, the saving of time, which was previously lost when moving from one operation to another; third, to the invention of a large number of machines that make work easier and reduce the time needed to do it, allowing one man to do the work of many."

Q - Professor Smith, what was the principle that gave rise to the division of labor?

A - "This division of labor, from which so many advantages derive, was not originally caused by human genius, intentionally foreseeing the wealth that it would provide. It was the necessary, albeit slow and gradual, consequence of a particular tendency in human nature that aims at a less extensive utility: the tendency to negotiate and exchange one thing for another."

Q - Professor Smith, you have said that the division of labor is limited by the extent of the market. How does this happen?

A - "As the exchanges are at the origin of the division of labor, the extent of these will always be limited by the extent of those or, in other words, by the extent of the market. When this is very restricted, no one feels willing to dedicate himself completely to a single task, as he cannot exchange all the surplus of his work, which he does not need, for the surplus of the production of other men, in which he is interested." [1]

Q - You have shown that the origin and use of currency are associated with people's need to make exchanges. With the implementation of the division of labor, the possibility of making exchanges, in your view, must have been frequently impeded or hindered, because the interests of exchange have not been made compatible, for example, between two specific people. At that moment, the currency allows these interests to be reconciled. Professor Smith, in this exchange process, what does the exchange value of a commodity represent to you?

A - "Each man is considered rich or poor according to his own with the possibility of acquiring the objects that are necessary and convenient for him and enjoying the pleasures of human life. After the division of labor has been implemented, only a small part of these objects can be obtained by each man through his own work; most of them are produced by the work of other people, which leads us to consider a man rich or poor according to the amount of work he can have at his disposal or can buy. Therefore, the value of any commodity, for the person who owns it, and who does not intend to use it or exchange it for others, is equal to the quantity of all commodities. The true price of anything, what it costs the man who intends to acquire it, is the toil and inconvenience he is forced to acquire (...) work was the first price, work was the first price, the first exchange currency that was paid for all things."

Q - So, for you, does the time needed to produce a product determine its value?

A - "In that primitive and rough state of society that precedes both the accumulation of goods and the appropriation of land, the proportion between the quantities of labor necessary to acquire the different objects seems to constitute the only circumstance that can provide a rule for the exchange of these same objects among themselves. If a nation of hunters, for example, kills a beaver that normally costs twice the labor required to kill a deer, that beaver should be exchanged for, or worth, two deer. It is logical that the product of two days or two hours of work is worth twice as much as what normally only requires a day or an hour of work."

Q - Professor Smith, although the inequality in the distribution of income has been pointed out by you as a reality of our time, the poorest have had access to better living conditions. Does this represent a new reality to be highlighted?

A - "The answer seems at first glance evident. Servants, workers and factory workers of different professions constitute most of the population of any political society. But what improves the conditions in which this majority of the population finds itself can never be considered as inconvenient for society. No society can flourish and be happy if most of its elements are poor and miserable. It is only fair that those who feed, dress and house the entire population are rewarded in such a way that they can also be reasonably fed, dressed and accommodated."

Q - Professor Smith, you have established a relationship between remuneration for work, marriage and birth rate and you have also seen the human species as a commodity. Could you explain to us how this relationship takes place?

A - "A generous reward from work, allowing workers to better educate their children and, therefore, reduce mortality, naturally tends to foster and expand those limits (proportion of children reaching maturity). It should be noted that this situation is necessarily dependent on the state of demand for work. If this demand increases continuously, the reward of work encourages marriage and the multiplication of workers so that they can supply this increase in demand with a continuous increase in the population (...) This is how the demand for men, like any other commodity, necessarily regulates the production of the human species."

Q - You have said that if a society let things go by themselves, with perfect freedom and where each man could freely decide which occupation would most interest him, the wages of a region and different industries would tend to be equivalent. However, in his view, some factors would contribute to this not happening. What factors are these?

A - "First, the fact that the work on them is pleasant or not; second, the degree of difficulty in learning each business, and the expense required to do so; third, the regularity or irregularity of the work guaranteed by these industries; fourth, the greater or lesser confidence that can be placed in those who exercise the profession; and fifth, the greater or lesser probability of succeeding in it."

Q - Professor Smith, you have been studying the determinants of land income. What does this income consist of?

A - "The rent, considered as the price paid for the use of the land, is naturally the highest possible that the tenant can pay given the characteristics of the land. When the owner adjusts the terms of the lease, he tries not to leave the tenant more than the percentage of profits necessary to replenish the capital necessary to buy the seeds, pay the labor, buy and keep livestock and other farming instruments, and the current profits from working capital in that region. This is, of course, the minimum percentage that the tenant can settle without losing, and the owner rarely intends to leave him more than that. The owner tries, of course, to reserve the part of the production as land rent or, what is the same, the part of the production price that exceeds this percentage, this rent being the highest that the tenant can afford given the characteristics from the earth. Sometimes liberality or, more frequently, the owner's ignorance leads him to accept an income below that portion; and sometimes also, albeit more rarely, the ignorance of the tenant leads him to commit to paying more, or to settling for a profit lower than the current profit of the capital on the exploitation in the region. That portion can, however, be considered as the natural income of the land, or income because it is generally considered that the land should be rented."

Q - But according to what factors does this income vary?

A - "The rent of the land not only varies according to its fertility, whatever its production, but also with its situation, whatever its fertility. Land located close to a city pays a higher rent than land that is equally fertile in a distant part of the countryside."

Q - Professor Smith, you have criticized mercantilists, given the importance they attach to the accumulation of precious metals. Can you explain this position?

A - "Most authors who collected the cash prices for various things in ancient times seem to have considered the low price of wheat and goods in general or, in other words, the high value of gold and silver, as a proof not only of the scarcity of these metals, but also of the poverty and barbarism of the times when such prices were practiced. This idea is related to the political economy system that considers that national wealth consists of abundance and national poverty in the scarcity of gold and silver, I will limit myself for now to observe that the high value of precious metals is not proof of poverty or barbarism in each country at the time. It is just a testament to the sterility of the mines that currently supplied the commercial world. Not only can a poor country not buy larger quantities of gold and silver, but it is impossible to pay more for these metals; their value will therefore not be higher in the former than in the latter. In China, a country much richer than any part of Europe, the value of precious metals is much higher than in any part of Europe. Just as Europe's wealth has increased dramatically since the discovery of America's mines, so has the value of gold and silver gradually decreased."

Q - But what is the reason for this decrease in the value of gold and silver?

A - "This decrease in the value of precious metals should not, however, be attributed to the increase in Europe's real wealth, annual production, land and labor, but rather to the accidental discovery of mines, more abundant than all that until then were known (...) The amount of precious metals can increase in any country for two different reasons: first, due to the greater abundance of mines from which they are extracted; secondly, due to the increase in the wealth of these people, a consequence of the increase in the production of their annual work. The first of these causes is necessary and undoubtedly correlates with a decrease in the value of these metals, but the second does not."

Q - Professor Smith, you have said that progress causes a drop in the price of manufactured products. Could you explain to us how this happens?

A - "It is a natural effect of the improvements to gradually reduce the real price of almost all manufactured products. The price of labor required for its manufacture may decrease in all, without exception. As a result of better machinery, greater dexterity and a better division of labor, all natural effects of improvement, a much smaller amount of work is required for the execution of any work, and without, as a result of the state flourishing society, the real price of labor will rise very considerably, however this large decrease in the amount of labor will more than generally compensate for the greatest possible price increase." [2]

Q - For you, a civilized society consists of three classes. What classes are these?

A - "The total annual production of land and labor in any country or, which means the same thing, the total price of this annual production is naturally divided, as we have already seen, into three parts: land rent, labor wages, and working capital profits; and it constitutes the income of three kinds of people: those who live on income, those who live on wages, and those who live on profits. It is these three classes that originally make up the entire civilized society, and whose income ultimately derives from those of all other classes."

Q - Professor Smith, is it true that you consider Traders and Industrialists to be more intelligent than landowners?

A - "The merchants and bosses of manufactures are (...) the two types of people who usually invest more capital, and who, due to their wealth, are generally more heard by public authorities. As they spend their whole lives making plans and projects, they often have a more developed intelligence than most rural landowners (...) The superiority they have over rural landowners lies not so much in knowing the interests of society in general, as before when they have a better knowledge of their own interests than the rural man has of theirs."

Q - You have said that the interests of entrepreneurs are conflicting with the interests of the public and that it is in the interests of entrepreneurs to eliminate competition. Why is that?

A - "Traders are always interested in changing markets and eliminating competition. The enlargement of the markets may coincide with the interests of the public, but the elimination of competition will always be detrimental to it, and can only favor traders, raising their profits above the natural sectors, and imposing an absurd tax on their benefit over the rest of the population. Any proposal for a new law or regulation issued by this class must be viewed with suspicion, never being adopted without a long and careful examination, carried out with suspicious attention. It comes from a class of men whose interests never coincide at all with those of the public, which in general consists of deceiving and even oppressing the general public, and who have consequently deceived and oppressed him many times." [3]

Q - There is some confusion about the differentiation between natural price and market price. Could you tell us what each one means?

A - "There is a normal or average index of wages for each line of work and capital profit in all communities or regions. This index is naturally regulated, as I will demonstrate, by the general conditions of the community, its wealth or poverty, its progress, its stationary situation or its decline and, on the other hand, by the nature of each type of work. There is also a normal or average income index in each community or region, which is also regulated, as I will demonstrate, by the general conditions of the community in the region where the land is located and by its natural or artificial fertility. These normal or average rates can be referred to as natural rates of wages, profit and income, in the time and place to which they correspond. When the price of any commodity is neither higher nor lower than enough to pay the rent of the land, the wages of labor and the profits of the capital employed in the harvest, preparation and transportation of the commodity to the market, according to its indexes such goods are said to be sold at their natural price. The commodity is then sold precisely for what it is worth, that is, for what it costs the person who places it on the market (...) The price at which any commodity is actually sold is called the market price. It can be higher, lower or exactly equal to the natural price. The market price of a given commodity is regulated by the ratio between the quantity of that commodity on the market and the demand for those who wish to pay it at the natural price, that is, the total amount paid for the income, labor and profit that it is necessary to spend to put it on the market."

Q - You have said that a society's capital stock increases with savings and decreases with lavishness and extravagant spending. Could you explain it better?

A - "What a person saves from his income is added to that person's capital, which either invests directly, keeping a larger number of productive hands, or lends it to others with interest, that is, through a percentage of the profits, thus allowing that other person to keep with that capital a greater number of productive hands. Just as the capital of an individual can only increase by saving a part of his income or his annual gain, so the capital of a company, which consists of the sum of the capital of all the individuals that compose it, can only increase from that the same way."

Q - You have said that the city industry is largely benefited from the field industry. How does this happen?

A - "The superiority that the city industry enjoys in every corner of Europe over that of the countryside is not just about corporations and their laws: it is also based on many other regulations. The heavy taxes imposed on foreign manufactures and on goods imported by merchants tend to reinforce this situation. Corporate laws allow city dwellers to increase their prices, without fearing the possibility of facing any competition with peasants; those other regulations still allow them to have no problems with possible competition from foreign countries."

Q - Professor Smith, you introduced the concept of surplus value before Marx, although you did not use that term. How do you think the capital accumulation mechanism works in capitalist economies?

A - "When goods are accumulated in the hands of private individuals, some of them will naturally use this reserve in recruiting skilled people, to whom they will provide materials and means of subsistence with a view to making a profit by selling their work, that is, hoping that the value of this work will add to that of those materials. When exchanging the manufactured object for money, labor or other goods, for a price higher than what is necessary to pay for the used materials and the workers' wages, something must remain for the person who risked his reserve of goods in this adventure. The value that workers add to the materials, therefore, is divided in this case, into two parts, one of which pays their wages and the other constitutes the profits, of the one who employed it, on the material reserves and advance wages." [4]

Q - Professor Smith, you created a concept that is considered the backbone of your economic thinking, which is the concept of the "invisible hand". What does the invisible hand mean and what is its relation to the public interest?

A - "(...) since everyone seeks, as far as possible, to use his capital to promote the activity (...) and to direct this activity in such a way that his product has the maximum possible value, each individual necessarily strives to increase society's annual income as much as possible. Generally, in reality, he does not intend to promote the public interest, nor does he know to what extent he is promoting it (...) In using his capital, he has only his own security in mind; when orienting its activity in such a way that its production can be of greater value, it aims only at its own gain and, in this, as in many other cases, it is taken as if by an invisible hand to promote an objective that was not part of its intentions. In fact, it is not always worse for society that this objective is not part of the individual's intentions. In pursuing his own goals, the individual often promotes the interest of society much more effectively than how much he really intends to promote it."

## 2.3. Author's Notes

[1] The globalization and expansion of multinational companies throughout the second half of the 20th century and the beginning of the 21st century, expands on an unprecedented scale, the division of labor and, therefore, the productivity and profit of these companies, making them an overwhelming power.

[2] It is a fact that the price of goods with a high technological content has dropped substantially over the last few decades (mobile phones, digital cameras, computers, televisions, etc.), and this fact can be associated with Adam Smith's idea that the smallest quantity the labor factor leads to lower prices.

[3] Business behavior over the past two centuries shows that Adam Smith was right when he said that entrepreneurs are always interested in eliminating competition, as the concentration of capital has systematically increased worldwide and can be understood as a policy of capitalist companies.

[4] Here Adam Smith establishes a clear relationship between the profits of entrepreneurs and the risk they take; that is, profit, in the modern view, is seen as the remuneration of business risk.

# 3. An "Interview" with Karl Marx (1818-1883)

"Philosophers have interpreted the world differently, but it is important to change it."

(Karl Marx)

Karl Marx (1818-1883)

## 3.1. Who Was Karl Marx

Karl Marx, economist, philosopher and socialist, was born in Trier, Germany, on May 5, 1818, dying on March 14, 1883, in London, England. A student at the University of Berlin, he had a special interest in Hegelian philosophy, graduating in 1841 with the thesis "On the Differences between the Philosophy of Nature of Democritus and Epicurus". [1]

When he took over as editor of the Rheinische Zeitung (Rhineland News) in 1842, in Cologne, Marx started to articulate a series of radical-democratic ideas, leading him to fret with the authorities and forcing him to move to France (Paris), where, from 1844, he edited the "German-French Annals", the main vehicle of the left Hegelians, whose main leaders were Bruno Bauer and Ruge and with whom he soon broke off.

A friendship initiated in Paris in 1844 will have enormous importance throughout his life: the friendship of Friedrich Engels (1820-1895), with which he published the leaflet "The Communist Manifesto", on February 24, 1848, after he was expelled from France in 1845, based in Brussels, where he joined clandestine workers' organizations and political exiles. This leaflet represents the embryonic ideas of the revolutionary theory that would become the doctrine called "Marxism".

Friedrich Engels (1820-1895)

With the defeat of revolutionary movements in Europe and the closing of the newspaper, Marx returns to Paris, from where he is expelled again, going to London, where he took up residence and where he would die. It is in this city, as a frequent visitor to the British Museum, that Marx will develop his main ideas that culminated in the publication of the first volume of "Capital", in 1867, a fundamentally economic book analyzing the theories of value, surplus value and accumulation of capital, among other topics, containing vast documentation that, in Marx's view, demonstrated all the contradiction of the capitalist system.

Marxism, as a political theory, tries to explain universal history as a history of class struggle, and capitalism, in Marx's view, in the face of its own contradictions, would tend to disappear after the proletarian revolution.

The sociological basis of Marxist theory deals with the alienation of man by the mechanism of production and the division of labor (already studied by Adam Smith and whom Marx criticizes).

# 3.2. Marxism and the Exploitation of Man by Man

Marxism is a doctrine based on the thought and doctrine of socialist theorists, the German philosophers Karl Marx (1818-1883) and Friedrich Engels (1820-1895), notably in the revolutionary works "Capital", published in 1867, and "Communist Manifesto", published in 1848.

In his analysis, Marx rejects not only idealism as a philosophical principle, but also the doctrine of David Hume (1711-1776) and Immanuel Kant (1724-1804). The old materialism, as seen by Marx (and by Engels), conceived of the "human essence" as abstract and as the "set of social relations", only interpreting the world, when in reality it would be necessary to transform it; that is, Marx attaches great importance to "practical revolutionary action". [2] [3]

From 1844, when his philosophical ideas were consolidated, Marx became a materialist and a follower of the philosopher Ludwig Andreas von Feuerbach (1804-1872). Regarding the materialist conception of history, Engels (in the work "Ludwig Feuerbach"), a friend and coauthor of Marx wrote: "The great cardinal problem of all philosophy, especially modern, is the problem of the relationship between thinking and being, between spirit and nature (...) Which came first, spirit or nature? (...) Philosophers were divided into two major fields, according to the challenge they gave to this question. Those who affirmed the anteriority of the spirit vis-à-vis nature, those who, therefore, ultimately admitted a creation of the world, of whatever class (...) were grouped in the field of idealism. The others, those for whom nature was the first, trained in the different schools of materialism."

**Ludwig Andreas von Feuerbach (1804-1872)**

In the Marxist view, throughout life, human beings subject themselves, involuntarily, to certain relations of production that would correspond to a certain stage of development of their material productive forces. The set of these relations of production constitutes the economic infrastructure of society, the material base on which the superstructure is built (legal, political, philosophical, cultural, social, spiritual ideological basis) and to which certain forms of social consciousness correspond. For Marx, the mode of production of material life influences the process of social, political and spiritual life in general; that is, it is not the consciousness of the human being that determines his being, but it is the social being that determines his conscience. Upon reaching a certain stage of development, the material productive forces of society clash with the existing relations of production, that is, with the relations of property in which they were formed. It is from here, according to Marx, that these relations cease to be agents favorable to the productive forces, to become adversaries of these forces, opening the doors to the social revolution. Thus, by changing the material economic base, the entire ideological superstructure that was built on it is revolutionized.

Marx begins his analysis of the capitalist system with the analysis of the commodity. According to Marx, the commodity is, above all, an object that satisfies a human need. It is also an object that can be exchanged for another. Therefore, a commodity can have two types of value: use value and exchange value. The usefulness of a commodity transforms it into use value. The exchange value, however, is nothing more than the ratio or proportion in which a certain number of use values of one species are exchanged for a certain number of use values of another species. For Marx, the different goods have in common the fact that they are the result of human work. In this sense, the production of goods is a system of social relations in which different producers produce different products - from the social division of labor - and in which these products are equivalent to each other through exchange. Thus, the common point for all commodities is human labor. Each commodity individually represents simply a certain amount of socially necessary labor time to produce it. In this way, the magnitude of the value is determined by the amount of socially necessary labor or the socially necessary labor time to produce a certain commodity or use value. Fundamentally, goods are simply amounts of time spent on them.

In the Marxist perspective, the advancement of the socialization of work, which is manifested in the development of the great production of capitalist companies, increasingly concentrated and cartelized, and in the immense growth of financial capital, is the most important material basis of, for Marx, inevitable emergence of socialism. The driving force behind this transformation is the proletarian class, formed and trained by the capitalist system itself. Their struggle against the bourgeoisie turns into a political struggle for the conquest of political power that would lead to the "dictatorship of the proletariat". The socialization of production would lead to the transformation of the means of production into social property, that is, the "expropriation of expropriators". In this logic, the considerable increase in labor productivity, the reduction of working hours and the replacement of the small business unit by collective work would be direct consequences of this process.

In analyzing the role of the state, Marx concludes that nations are, at the same time, an inevitable product and form of development of bourgeois society. In the Marxist view, the working class could not develop without "organizing itself within the limits of the nation"; that is, without being "national". However, the development of capitalism would destroy national barriers, end national isolation and replace national conflicts with world class conflicts. For Marx, in advanced capitalist countries workers have no homeland and "the common action" of workers, at least in so-called developed countries, "is one of the first conditions for their emancipation", as expressed in the "Communist Manifesto" and the famous slogan Marxist: "Workers of the world unite".

Within the Marxist logic, the transformation of capitalist to socialist society would be inevitable, based on the economic law of the movement of modern society with the development of new forms of production, new organization of the family and the new role of women in society. Thus, social changes would set in motion the mechanism that would lead to the social revolution and, ultimately, the collapse of the capitalist system itself and the rise of socialism.

Marx's central thesis is that capitalism is sustained in the exploitation of the working class, which receives only the amount corresponding to the replacement of its labor force, that is, it receives only enough to acquire the goods necessary to keep itself alive and reproduce as a species.

Marx created the concept of surplus value, the meaning of which had already been developed by Adam Smith (1723-1790) in "The Wealth of Nations". The surplus value is the source of capital accumulation in the capitalist system, being the result of capitalist exploitation. In the Marxist conception, surplus value is generated by obtaining a higher use value than the payment received by workers, that is, the difference between the value of the goods produced and the payment of the value of the labor force used.

Marx can be considered a disciple of David Ricardo (1772-1832), adopting, in addition to other concepts, his theory of value. In fact, Marx also uses Adam Smith's concept of exchange value. Combining this theory with his theory of surplus value, Marx developed a theory of the reproduction of capital in the capitalist system, based on the exploitation of the working class. This exploitation would lead, in the long run, to the inevitable class conflict, the seed of the working-class revolution. As a result, workers would remove their instrument of exploitation from the capitalists - the control of the means of production - placing it under the rule of the State, leading to the collectivization of the means of production ("the expropriation of expropriators"). Thus, a new model of production would appear, called Socialism. [4]

David Ricardo (1772-1832)

The relations of production existing in the capitalist system and the resulting legal superstructure determine that the surplus value is appropriated by the bourgeois class, the owners of the means of production. The forces of the system lead the ruling class to a continuous accumulation of capital, causing a reduction in the rate of profits due to the increasing concentration of capital. In parallel, progressive mechanization creates a permanent industrial reserve army that keeps wages at the subsistence level. In the Marxist conception, the concentration of capital and the organization of production by the industry of mass structures of workers disciplined and trained by the system itself will lead to the social revolution.

Marxism focuses on dialectical materialism, which developed from the theories of class struggle that resulted in the creation of the theory and tactics of the proletarian revolution. Dialectical materialism is the fundamental doctrine of Marxism, having as its main foundation the idea that the world is constituted by a process in which everything is in perpetual movement and transformation, nothing being finished and ready. Historical materialism, in turn, is the doctrine originated in Marxism that states that the set of processes (social, political and economic) is conditioned by the mode of material production.

There are two important philosophical concepts associated with Marxism: socialism and communism. Socialism is the doctrine that defends the prevalence of the interests of society over individual interests, removing individual action from the scene and replacing collective action in the production of goods and services and in the distribution of income and wealth. There are two fundamental and divergent strands in socialism: scientific socialism and utopian socialism.

Scientific socialism is based on the doctrine of historical materialism, proposing the nationalization of the means of production. Utopian socialism is opposed to scientific socialism and is based on idealistic government programs and not on economic reality itself. Examples of utopian socialists in the 19th century were Robert Owen (1771-1858), Claude Henri de Rouvroy, comte de Saint-Simon (1760-1825) and François Marie Charles Fourier (1772-1837).

Communism, on the other hand, is based on state control of the means of production, with the elimination of private property, being seen as a step after socialism.

The Russian Revolution of 1917, led by Vladimir Ilych Ulianov or Lenin (1870-1924), resulted in the implementation, in practice, of Marxist theories, centered on the formation of an economic system that would use state ownership of the means of production, the collectivization of land and centralized planning.

## 3.3. Marx's Theory of Work Value and the Collapse of the Capitalist System

Marx was substantially interested in the questions of the class struggle of the proletariat and, according to him, the history of all societies that existed is the history of class struggles ("Communist Manifesto"). In this view, capitalism would be centered on the exploitation of the working classes by capitalists.

Marx develops the concept of surplus value to explain the process of capital accumulation and the exploitation of workers in the capitalist system. To extract surplus value, the money holder needs to find in the market a commodity whose use value has the unique property of being also a source of value, that is, a commodity whose consumption process is also a process of value creation. In Marxist analysis, this commodity is man's labor force and there would be two fundamental ways to increase surplus value: by increasing the working day (absolute surplus) and reducing the necessary working time (relative surplus).

The control of the means of production on the part of the capitalist class, forced workers to sell their labor power for less than their contribution to the value of production, generating, for Marx, capitalist exploitation. Marx, in analyzing the production of relative surplus value, investigates the three fundamental historical stages in the process of intensifying labor productivity in the capitalist system: 1) simple cooperation; 2) division of labor and manufacturing; 3) machines and large industry.

In Marx's work-value theory, the value of goods is subdivided into three elements, as shown in the expression below:

$$V = c + v + s$$

Where:
V = Value.
c = constant capital (machinery).
v = variable capital (labor).

s = surplus value.

From the previous equation it is possible to extract the following relationships:

$$\frac{s}{v} = surplus\ value\ rate\ (capitalist\ exploitation\ rate)$$

$$\frac{c}{v} = organic\ capital\ composition$$

$$\frac{s}{c+v} = rate\ of\ profit$$

# 3.4. The Collapse of Capitalism

In the Marxist analysis, the fastest growth of constant capital (in the total sum of capital) vis-à-vis variable capital is of fundamental importance in the process of development of capitalism and its transformation into socialism. By replacing workers (variable capital) with machinery (constant capital), capitalism would generate wealth for some (capitalists) and misery for others (workers). The accumulation of capital generates what Marx called the reserve industrial army, that is, the relative surplus of workers that allows capital to increase production. In the Marxist perspective, the combination of credit and the process of capital accumulation would explain the crises of overproduction that occur from time to time in capitalist countries.

The increase in labor productivity would lead to an increase in the constant capital / variable capital ratio. However, since the generation of surplus value depends on the share of variable capital in total capital, the share of profits in capital would tend to fall, leading to the rate of capital accumulation in the capitalist system tending to fall, which, in the perspective Marxist, would be one of the factors that would lead to the collapse of the capitalist system.

It is possible to identify in the Marx model the relationship between capital accumulation and the labor market in a capitalist economy, leading to the idea that the growth of wealth produced by work leads to an increase in unemployment:

"With the accumulation of capital produced by itself, the working population produces (...), in increasing volume, the means of its own relative redundancy. This is a population law peculiar to the capitalist mode of production". Karl Marx, The Capital, vol. 1, SP: Abril Cultural, 1984, p.20.

# 3.5. An "Interview" with Karl Marx

Q - Mr. Marx, in your critical analysis of capitalism, you begin with the analysis of the "commodity" which, in your view, has two kinds of value: use value and exchange value. Why did you choose the "commodity" to start your work?

A - "The wealth of societies, where capitalist production rules, is configured in "immense accumulation of goods", and merchandise, considered in isolation, is the elementary form of this wealth. Therefore, our investigation begins with the analysis of the merchandise. The commodity is, first, an external object, something that, due to its properties, satisfies human needs, whatever their nature, their origin, comes from the stomach or from fantasy (...) The variety of patterns of measurement of the goods stems from the diverse nature of the objects to be measured and also from convention. The usefulness of a thing makes it a use value (...) Use value is only realized with use or consumption. Use values constitute the material content of wealth, whatever its social form. In the form of society we are going to study, use values are, at the same time, the material vehicles of exchange value. The exchange value is revealed, at first, in the quantitative relationship between use values of different species, in the proportion in which they are exchanged, a relationship that constantly changes in time and space (...) Any commodity is exchanged for others, in the most diverse proportions (...) Take two commodities, for example, wheat and iron. Whatever the proportion in which they are exchanged, it is always possible to express it with an equality (...) As use values, goods are, first of all, of different qualities; as exchange values, they can only differ in quantity and therefore contain no atom of use value."

Q - Mr. Marx, You often say that goods have a secret, a fetish. What is that?

A - "At first glance, the merchandise seems to be a trivial thing, immediately understandable. Analyzing it, one sees that it is something very strange, full of metaphysical subtleties and theological quirks. As a use value, there is nothing mysterious about it, whether we observe it from the point of view that it is intended to satisfy human needs, with its properties as a result of human work (...) The mysterious character of the commodity does not come from its value of use, nor of the determining factors of value (...) The mysterious character that the product of work presents when it takes the form of merchandise from which it comes? That form, of course. The equality of human labor is disguised in the form of the equality of the products of labor as values; the measure through the duration, the expenditure of the human labor force takes the form of the quantity of value of the products of labor; finally, the relationships between producers, in which the social character of their work is affirmed, take the form of a social relationship between the products of work. The commodity is mysterious simply because it masks the social characteristics of the work of men, presenting them as material characteristics and social properties inherent to the products of labor; for hiding, therefore, the relationship between the individual work of the producers and the total work, by reflecting it as an existing social relationship, apart from them, between the products of their own work (...) This fetishism in the world of goods stems from as the preceding analysis demonstrates, of the social character of the work that produces goods. "

Q - In your analysis, Mr. Marx, the money that came to accelerate the exchange system, ends up becoming capital for the capitalist in the process of circulation of goods. Could you explain to us how this happens?


A - "The circulation of goods is the starting point of capital. The production of goods and commerce, a developed form of circulation of goods, constitutes the historical conditions that give rise to capital. World trade and markets inaugurate the modern history of capital in the 16th century. If we put aside the material content of the circulation of goods, the exchange of different values of use, to consider only the economic forms engendered by this process of circulation, we will find money as the final product. This final product of the circulation of goods is the first form in which capital appears. Historically, in its origins, it is in the form of money that capital is confronted with real estate, such as cash fortune, merchant or user capital. But it is not necessary to go back to the historical origin of capital to verify that money is the first form in which it appears. This phenomenon unfolds daily in our eyes. All new capital, to begin with, enters the stage, appears in the market for goods, labor or money, in the form of money that, through certain processes, must become capital. Money that is just money is distinguished from money that is capital, through the difference in the form of circulation."

Q - But how does this happen?

A - "The simple form of circulation of goods is M-C-M, conversion of merchandise into cash and conversion of money into merchandise, sell to buy. Next to it, we find a second one that is specifically diverse, C-M-C, converting money into merchandise and converting merchandise into cash, buy to sell. The money that moves according to the latter circulation becomes capital, becomes capital and, through its destination, is capital."

Q – Mr. Marx, You returned to a point already raised by Adam Smith, which is the question of the capitalist appropriation of part of the workers' production. What does that mean for you, and how is it determined?

A - "The product, owned by the capitalist, is a use value, threads, shoes, etc. But, although shoes are useful for the march of society and our capitalist is a determined progressive, he does not manufacture shoes out of passion for shoes. In the production of goods, our capitalist is not driven by pure love of use values. It produces use values just for being and while they were a material substrate, holders of exchange value. It has two goals. First, it wants to produce a use value that has an exchange value, an article intended for sale, a commodity. And second, he wants to produce a commodity of a higher value than the combined value of the commodities necessary to produce them, that is, the sum of the values of the means of production and the labor force, by which he anticipated his good money on the market. In addition to a use value, it wants to produce merchandise, in addition to use value, value, and not only value, but also surplus value (surplus value)."

Q - Some European unions and even political forces in Brazil have been demanding a reduction in working hours, without reducing wages. How do you see this issue?

A - "The establishment of a normal working day is the result of a multi-century struggle between the capitalist and the worker."

Q - John Stuart Mill (1806-1873) said that it is doubtful whether technological innovations have contributed to reducing workers' sacrifices. What do you think about it?

A - "This is not the objective of capital when it uses machinery. This job, like any other development of the productive force of labor, has the purpose of cheapening the goods, shortening the part of the working day that the worker needs for himself, to expand the other part that he gives to the capitalist free of charge. The machinery is a means to produce added value."

Q - Mr. Marx, the social and economic effects of the implementation of the mechanization of agriculture and the robotization of factories are currently being discussed. Do you think that these effects are negative for workers, or can they be positive in view of the compensation resulting from the increase in the efficiency of the economy and the possible reduction in the working day?

A - "The real facts, hidden by economic optimism, are these: the workers dismissed by the machine are transferred from the factory to the labor market and there the number of labor forces that are at the disposal of capitalist exploitation increases (...) This effect of the machine that was presented in the form of compensation for the working class, plagues it, on the contrary, in the most terrible way. For now, it is enough to say the following: workers made redundant from an industrial branch can undoubtedly seek employment in any other occupation. If they find it, thus rebuilding the link that existed between them and the means of subsistence from which they were dissociated, this happens through a new additional capital that seeks application, and in no way through the capital that it already expected before and became machine. Even in this case, their possibilities are slim. Atrophied by the division of labor, these poor devils are worth so little outside their scope of activity, that they only find access in inferior branches of work and, therefore, overcrowded to underpaid. In addition, each industrial branch attracts a new flow of human beings each year, the contingent to replace and increase its workers according to their regularly renewed needs. When the machinery dismisses part of the workers employed in a certain industrial branch, the contingent that flows to it is redistributed and absorbed by other branches, while the dismissed people largely ruin themselves and perish in the transition period."

Q - So, Mr. Marx, You attribute to technological changes the increase in unemployment?

A - "It is indisputable that the machinery itself is not responsible for the workers being stripped of their means of subsistence. It cheapens and increases the product in the branch that it takes over and, at first, it does not change the amount of subsistence produced in other branches. After its introduction, therefore, society has the same or greater means of subsistence for the dismissed workers, not taking into account the enormous portion of the annual product, which is dilapidated by those who are not workers. And this is the critical point of economic apology. For her, the inseparable contradictions and antagonisms of capitalist application in machinery do not exist, simply because they do not stem from machinery, but from its capitalist application."

**Q - Could you explain it better, Mr. Marx?**

**A -** "Machinery, as an instrument, increases working time, facilitates work, is a victory for man over natural forces, increases the wealth of those who actually produce, but, with capitalist application, generates opposite results: it prolongs working time increases its intensity, enslaves man through natural forces, impoverishes real producers."

**Q - But Mr. Marx, will not the increase in production due to the use of machines have an inductive effect on the use of labor in other sectors, increasing employment?**

**A -** "Although machinery necessarily dismisses workers in the branches where it is introduced, it can cause job increases in other branches. However, this effect has nothing in common with the so-called compensation theory. Since every product on the machine, one meter of machine-made cloth, for example, is cheaper than the manual product of the species, which has been supplanted, it is an absolute law: if the total quantity of the machine-made item remains equal to the total quantity of the item it replaces, produced by handicraft or manufacture, will decrease the total labor employed. The additional work required to produce the means of work, machinery, coal, etc., must be less than the decrease in work resulting from the application of the machine. Otherwise, the machine-made product would be as expensive or more expensive than the manual product. But the total quantity of the machine-made article with the lowest number of workers, instead of remaining equal to the total quantity of the deleted manual article, increases far beyond that quantity."

**Q – Mr. Marx, You have stated that the existence of an industrial reserve army is essential for the development of modern industry. Could you explain this concept better?**

**A -** "(...) In all branches, the increase in variable capital, that is, the number of workers employed is always associated with violent fluctuations and the transient formation of overpopulation. Due to the more forceful process of repulsion of workers already employed, or at least visible, but no less real, of the more difficult absorption of the additional working population through the usual channels. With the magnitude of the social capital already in operation and without great growth, with the expansion of the scale of production and the mass of mobilized workers, with the development of labor productivity, with the broader and more complete flow of the sources of wealth, it expands the scale on which workers' greatest attraction to is linked to their greatest repulsion. In addition, the speed of changes in the organic composition of capital and in its technical form increases, and an increasing number of branches of production are affected, simultaneously or alternatively, by these changes. For this reason, the working population, when producing the accumulation of capital, produces, in increasing proportions, the means that make it, relatively, a superfluous population. This is a law peculiar to the capitalist mode of production. In reality, every historical mode of production has its own population laws, valid within historical limits. (...) But if an excess working population is a necessary product of the accumulation or development of wealth in the capitalist system, it in turn becomes the lever of capitalist accumulation, and even a condition for the existence of the capitalist mode of production. It constitutes an industrial reserve army available, which belongs to capital as if it were created and maintained by it."

Q – Mr. Marx, You have stated that the average interest rate that is dominant in a country - as opposed to the ever-fluctuating market rates - is not determinable by any law. Could you explain it better?

A - "There is no such kind of natural interest rate in the sense that economists speak of a natural rate of profit and a natural rate of wages (...) And why one cannot infer from general laws the limits of average interest rate. The answer is simply in the nature of interest, it is only part of the average profit. The same capital appears in two aspects, as loan capital in the hands of the lender and as industrial or commercial capital in the hands of the capitalist - entrepreneur. But one, only once works and produces profit. In the production process, capital as loan capital plays no role. The way in which the two parties share this profit to which they are entitled is a fact that is purely empirical, belonging to the realm of chance, such as the sharing of the percentage fractions of the common profit of a commercial company by the respective partners. In the division between surplus value and salary - in which it essentially represents the determination of the profit rate - two totally different factors play a decisive role, labor force and capital. There we have functions of two independent variables that limit each other; and this qualitative difference results in the quantitative distribution of the value produced (...) The opposite happens with interest: the qualitative difference (...) derives from the purely quantitative distribution of the same amount of surplus value (...) average interest rates are constant in each country and over long periods, because the general rate of profit varies only over long periods - private rates of profit are constantly changing by opposite variations."

Q - Mr. Marx, if I understood the main feature of your argument to describe the mechanics of the capitalist system, it is from the transformation of money into capital that, with it, surplus value is produced. With surplus value, more capital is produced and, thus, we have designed the framework that shapes capitalist accumulation. The surplus value presupposes production on capitalist bases and, this, presupposes the existence of large amounts of capital and labor force in the hands of the producers of goods. However, could you show us, in more detail, how this capital accumulation materializes?

A - "We have seen how surplus value originates from capital and we will now see how capital is born out of surplus value. Application of surplus value as capital or conversion of surplus value into capital is what is called capital accumulation (...) The capital value was originally disbursed in the form of money; surplus value, on the contrary, exists, in its origin, as the value of a certain part of the gross product. If it is sold, transformed into cash, the value of capital regains its original form of existence. From that moment on, the value of capital and surplus value are amounts of money and their further conversion of capital is carried out in the same way. The capitalist uses both amounts in the purchase of goods that enable him to restart the manufacture of his article and this time on an expanded scale. But, to buy these goods you must find them on the market (...) Annual production must, first, provide all objects, use values, which will serve to replace the material elements of capital, consumed during the year. After deducting these elements, the surplus or liquid product in which the surplus value is characterized is left (...) To accumulate, it is necessary to transform part of the surplus product into capital. But, without doing miracles, only things that are applied in the work process, that is, means of production, and things that the worker needs to maintain himself, that is, means of subsistence, can be transformed into capital. As a result, part of the annual surplus labor has to be transformed to produce additional means of production and livelihood in excess of the amount needed to replace the advanced capital. In short, surplus value can only be transformed into capital because the surplus product, of which it is the value, already contains the material elements of a new capital (...) From a concrete point of view, accumulation does not pass reproduction of capital on a scale that grows progressively."

# 3.6. Author's Notes

### 3.6.1. Georg Wilhelm Friedrich Hegel (1770-1831)

Georg Wilhelm Friedrich Hegel (1770-1831) was a German philosopher deeply influenced by the works of Spinoza, Kant and Rousseau and by the developments of the French Revolution. The greatest representative of German idealism in the 19th century, Hegel deeply influenced Karl Marx's historical materialism.

Hegelian theory starts from the concept of totality, from absolute knowledge, from the idea of the end of history, from the deduction of all reality from the concept, from an identity in which there is no place for difference.

Hegel's followers were divided into two completely opposite groups: on the one hand, the so-called Hegelians on the right, his university disciples in Berlin, who defended Protestant orthodoxy in religion and political conservatism in politics; on the other hand, the Hegelians who interpreted Hegel in a revolutionary sense, characterized in religion by atheism and in politics by socialism. The main highlights in this group, in addition to Marx, were Bruno Bauer, Max Stirner, David Friedrich Strauss and Ludwig Feuerbach.

**Georg Wilhelm Friedrich Hegel (1770-1831)**

### 3.6.2. David Hume (1711-1776)

For David Hume (1711-1776), Scottish philosopher, man is characterized by a sense of "benevolence", in the sense of being useful for the orderly development of society. Hume influenced the thinking of Adam Smith, the father of economic liberalism, and analyzed the forces that drive economic activity, the desire for profit and accumulation. Hume was opposed to redistributive policies, considering that they were discouraging individual initiative, which were fundamental to the functioning of the economic system. He criticized mercantilists and physiocrats and attacked landowners because, in his view, they did not contribute to the increase of national wealth. Hume also studied monetary theory, interest theory, fiscal policy and international trade.

**David Hume (1711-1776)**

### 3.6.3. Immanuel Kant (1724-1804)

Kantism is the philosophical doctrine of Immanuel Kant (1724-1804), German philosopher, characterized by criticism that denies the possibility of a rational knowledge of the objects of metaphysics and religion, leading to the need to base morality on categorical imperatives created by practical reason. In turn, transcendental Idealism is Kant's philosophical doctrine, in which phenomena are considered not as things in themselves, but as simple representations.

Immanuel Kant (1724-1804)

The philosophical and political thought of liberalism defended by Montesquieu, Locke and Kant assumed that the division of powers would be the safeguard of the freedom of individuals in society. The tripartite theory of powers "as a principle of organization of the constitutional state" is a fundamental contribution of Montesquieu and Locke to political science, based on the principle that "power holds power".

### 3.6.4. David Ricardo (1772-1832)

David Ricardo (1772-1832), author of the book "Principles of Political Economy" is one of Adam Smith's most important disciples. Ricardo developed several original economic concepts, such as the "Iron Wages Law", according to which the lower the wages, the more difficult it will be for workers to feed large families, a fact that would prevent the collapse of humanity, as suggested by Thomas Malthus. David Ricardo was deeply interested in the issues of economic growth and, therefore, in the factors that explain the distribution of income.

David Ricardo (1772-1832)

Some of Ricardo's main contributions were:

- Developed the Iron Wages Law, which defended the idea that wages tended to be always close to the subsistence level, caused by the decrease in land productivity.
- Developed the Theory of the trend of falling profits in the long run.
- Predicted technological unemployment caused by technological progress and the deterioration of workers' living conditions, a fact that was later highlighted by Karl Marx.
- Changed the classic analysis of value.
- It showed the relationship between capital accumulation, economic expansion and income distribution.
- Studied international trade and defended free trade.
- Created the "Theory of Comparative Advantages", in which he suggested that if nations specialize in the production of goods in which they have comparative advantages, all will benefit from international trade, even if one of them is more efficient in the production of all goods. In 1817, David Ricardo published "Principles of Political Economy and Taxation", where he developed the theory of comparative advantages.

Ricardo is a radical liberal and incorporates the "Law of Say" in his works. However, in Ricardo's model, the rate of profit declines in the long run. The Ricardian mechanism works like this: the increase in population leads to the use of less and less fertile land for food production, raising food prices, which require more work for their production. Rising food prices lead to rising wages and falling profit rates. When this rate is equal to zero, the capital accumulation process breaks down leading to a steady state. According to Ricardo, however, there are two ways to prevent a steady state: the introduction of technical progress in agriculture; and the release of grain imports, which were made impossible by the Wheat Laws, which represented the interests of landowners in England. The importation of cheap cereals would prevent the rise in real wages, facilitating the increase in profits and the accumulation of fundamental capital for economic growth. In Adam Smith, capital accumulation would be stimulated by the increase in exports and the deepening of the division of labor.

Therefore, free trade is a sine qua non condition to the Ricardian economic theory, as it is the free import of cereals that will allow the expansion of the capital accumulation process. In addition, England's greater industrial development vis-à-vis other nations required the opening of markets for its products, being a natural route for the dominance of foreign markets by English products.

The passage, in his work, in which Ricardo defines the tendency for the profit rate to fall, is as follows:

"The natural tendency of profits, therefore, is to decrease, because, with the development of society and wealth, the additional quantity of food required is obtained with the sacrifice of more and more work". Ricardo, David, Principles of Political Economy and Taxation, Collection of Thinkers, SP: Abril Cultural, 1982, p. 97.

The importance of Ricardo's Land Income Theory is that it made it possible to analyze the long-term relationships between economic development and income distribution, based on the trend of declining capital accumulation and an increase in the share of national income belonging to landowners.

In his analysis of value, Ricardo equates value with the natural price, that is, the amount of labor necessary to produce the goods (past work + present work). Karl Marx, in turn, defines value as the socially necessary work for the production of the commodity, comprising constant capital + variable capital + surplus value.

Ricardo does not distinguish exchange values from production price, or natural price, for him similar concepts. According to Marx, however, the price of production and value are defined at different levels of abstraction, in which the price of production is obtained from a uniform rate of profit, calculated in value.

In David Ricardo's theory of value, the amount of labor incorporated is not the only determinant of the value of goods, and the value of the social product changes if the appropriate portions change for wages and profits.

# 4. An "Interview" with John Maynard Keynes (1883-1946)

"To transform the entrepreneur into a speculator is to strike capitalism because it destroys the psychological mechanism that allows the perpetuation of unequal rewards (...). The entrepreneur is only tolerable as long as it is possible to accept that his earnings have some relationship with what, grossly in any sense, his activities brought as a contribution to society".

Keynes (1883-1946)

John Maynard Keynes (1883-1946)

40

# 4.1. Who Was Keynes

English economist, John Maynard Keynes was born on June 5, 1883, in Cambridge, dying on April 21, 1946, in Firle, Sussex. After obtaining a doctorate in mathematics in Cambridge, Keynes serves two years in India as a Treasury official and, on his return to London, takes up public office. In 1915, Keynes became an official in the Ministry of Finance and, in 1919, he headed the British delegation to the Peace Conference. [1]

Since he did not agree with the economic policy imposed on Germany in the Treaty of Versailles, Keynes broke with the government in 1919, starting to teach political economics at the University where he received his doctorate. That same year, he wrote an article of great repercussion ("The Economic Consequences of Peace"), in which he points out the dangers for Europe resulting from the harsh measures imposed on Germany. [2]

Despite having his training based on classical economic theory, Keynes starts to develop ideas that accentuate his divergences with that theory, manifested in the criticisms that he starts to make to the government, particularly in relation to the policy of deflation. In 1923, he published "Treaty on Monetary Reform"; in 1925, he published "Economic Consequences of Winston Churchil" and, in 1930, he published "Treaty on Currency".

However, it was in 1936 that Keynes published his most important work ("General Theory of Employment, Interest and Money"), which came to play a role of unparalleled importance in economic literature and to serve as a guide for most capitalist countries since its publication.

After going through the hard years of the "Great Depression", capitalist economies were looking for the solution to the problems of high unemployment and low production. For orthodox economists, unemployment was due to pressure on workers for wages. Keynes, in his work, proved that it was exactly the opposite, inasmuch as wage flattening implied insufficient aggregate demand that led to falling prices, overproduction (not explained by classical theory) and unemployment.

For Keynes, the stimulus to the expansion of aggregate demand (whose insufficiency caused unemployment) could be achieved with the intervention of the State in the economic domain, through fiscal policies that would trigger public investments that, in his opinion, would generate multiplier effects on the rest of the economy, increasing aggregate demand, stimulating private investment and thus leading the economy to full employment. In this sense, the role of the State would not be to occupy the spaces of the private sector, but only to act as a regulator of aggregate demand, stimulating it in depressive phases and reducing it in phases of excessive demand.

Representative of the United Kingdom at the Bretton Woods Conference in 1944, Keynes presents a program in which he defended the end of gold-based agreements, the international stabilization of the currency and the creation of an International Monetary Fund, an institution that was created that same year and of which he was appointed director, in 1946. [3] [4] [5]

Weeks after having strong friction with the Secretary of Finance of the United States, at the first meeting of the International Monetary Fund, for disagreeing with some decisions made, Keynes dies victimized by a heart attack, bequeathing to future generations an important job, even called revolutionary, showing that the State, as long as it acts correctly and at the right time, can be an important corrective instrument for the cycles proper to the capitalist system and, thus, not only protecting it, but also boosting it.

# 4.2. Historical Evolution of Macroeconomics

Until the 1930s, the concepts of microeconomics and macroeconomics did not exist as defined today. In fact, there was no distinction between microeconomics and macroeconomics. What existed was Economic Theory, notably the concept of Political Economy, which involved concepts now considered microeconomic or macroeconomic, with absolute predominance of neoclassical economic principles, Marxism representing the only real challenge to these principles.

The practical use of liberal marginalist principles reigned absolutely until the beginning of the First World War, when it was replaced by a planning system in warmongering countries. This change had strategic reasons and aimed to know the economic and military capabilities of the belligerent countries. However, it is with the Great Depression in the 1930s, that these principles fall to the ground, using state intervention mechanisms in the economic domain ("New Deal", for example, in 1934, in the United States), notably from the publication of Keynes' book "General Theory" in 1936. Thus, state intervention becomes one of the instruments of economic policy in capitalist countries.

Therefore, the separation between microeconomics and macroeconomics took place in the 1930s, mainly with the development of macroeconomics, after the publication of Keynes' "General Theory" in 1936. The concepts developed and/or perfected by Keynes become the macroeconomics, in a collective view of the world, while the rest of economic theory, the marginalist base, starts to constitute microeconomics, in an individualist view of the world. Keynes, in his classic work, separates the micro and macroeconomic concepts in the following passage:

"The division of economics into the theory of value and distribution on the one hand and the theory of currency on the other seems to me to be false. The correct dichotomy is, in my view, between the theory of industry or the individual company and the remuneration and distribution of each quantity of resources among different uses, on one part, and the theory of production and employment as a whole, otherwise." J. M. Keynes, The General Theory of Employment, Interest and Currency, Nova Cultural, 1985, p. 203.

# 4.3. The Formation of Macroeconomics

As we saw earlier, Macroeconomics was not recognized as an economic discipline before the 1930s. Some factors were decisive for the development of Macroeconomics:

• The collection and systematization of aggregated data provided the scientific basis for macroeconomic research. The collection of aggregated information from the First World War was the starting point of this process, as many countries felt the need to monitor the economic performance of adversary and/or enemy countries in the international scenario, to be able to assess the points of their strengths and weaknesses. Subsequently, the NBER - National Bureau of Economic Research, a private research institution in the United States, carried out an important and pioneering work of data collection and analysis in the 1920s, led by Simon Kuznets (1901-1985), Ukrainian economist naturalized American, who would be awarded the Nobel Prize in Economics in 1971 for his empirically grounded analyzes of economic growth. By the 1930s, the United States had a series of data on national income accounts, which would later be used to study trends at the macroeconomic level. Kuznets contributed decisively to the development of national accounting techniques by raising the problems arising from the measurement of large economic aggregates.

Simon Kuznets (1901-1985)

• Studies by Wesley Clair Mitchell (1874-1948), a prominent member of the American institutionalist school, showed that the US economy was subject to business cycles in which variables such as stocks, production and prices tended to undergo systematic changes over a typical business cycle.

**Wesley Clair Mitchell (1874-1948)**

• The Great Depression, which started in 1929, was characterized by a huge decline in economic activity, which led to an unprecedented increase in the unemployment rate. In the early 1930s, approximately 25 percent of American workers were unable to find work. The Great Depression represented, in practice, the questioning of classical economic principles, especially the famous Say's Law, which assumed that the natural forces of the market would avoid long-term and large-scale unemployment. John Maynard Keynes put Macroeconomics on the modern path by proposing a new theoretical framework for explaining the Great Depression and suggesting specific governmental measures to counteract the economic depression.

**Jean Baptiste Say (1767-1832)**

Macroeconomics, in fact, was developed from the base of Microeconomics developed by marginalist or neoclassical

45

economists in the 19th century. Microeconomics studies the isolated decisions of millions of firms and consumers that end up generating general economic trends, that is, macroeconomics. Therefore, the macroeconomic basis comes from microeconomics, since it studies, at a theoretical level, the decision-making processes of companies and consumers. Macroeconomic models assume that in the economy there is a firm or average consumer or representative of the entire economy and that, therefore, it has the characteristics of the average economy.

Macroeconomics studies the general behavior of the economy adding all the decisions of consumers and firms trying to establish the relationships between the economic variables studied.

Macroeconomics defines theoretical principles and, from data collection, gives empirical content to the theory, collecting and testing the validity of a proposed theoretical relationship, to measure a relationship quantitatively, to explain the past of an economy, or to arrive at a certain economic forecast for the future.

In macroeconomics there is a strong interaction between the positive economy and the normative economy, insofar as there is a great concern both with the establishment of a rigorous theoretical structure and with policies that lead to the improvement of social well-being.

# 4.4. Keynes' Contribution

Keynes was the first economist to consistently explain the Great Depression, attaching fundamental importance to the instability of private investor confidence in explaining this phenomenon. Keynes's main contributions to Macroeconomic Theory (see, for example, Simonsen & Cysne, Macroeconomics, 1995) are:

• Organized the basic concepts of national accounting, which would eventually lead to the emergence of modern Macroeconomics.

• Elaborated, in detail, the operation of the capitalist economy in the absence of the "Walrasian auctioneer" and realized that, in the impossibility of all markets being in balance, Walras's identity was not a valid economic principle. Therefore, the non-validity of Walras's identity also implied the invalidity of Say's Law, which stated that supply generated its own demand, if the free market would naturally avoid large-scale unemployment. For Keynes, Say's Law would only work in markets that operate on a barter system, that is, in an economy where there is no currency. This question had already been discussed by Malthus (1766-1834). [6]

• Concluded that there is resistance to falling nominal wages; that there is an important relationship between the interest rate and the demand for currency; and created the consumption function.

• Built, for the first time, models of aggregate economic balance in the short term.

• Introduced the concept of compensatory fiscal policy, in which recessions would result from the lack of private investments to absorb the savings generated at the height of the cycle. For Keynes, the public deficit should be counter-cyclical (for the classics it should be balanced).

• Defended government intervention as an instrument of economic policy to solve the problems arising from low effective demand, rescuing interventionist mercantilist principles.

• Introduced the concept of effective demand within a macroeconomic perspective. The Keynesian multiplier describes the increase in effective demand in a decelerating capitalist economy. Keynes emphasized the role of aggregate demand in macroeconomic fluctuations. The creation of the term "effective demand" is attributed to Thomas Malthus (1766-1834) in his classic 1820 work ("Principles of Political Economy").

In the book "General Theory of Employment, Interest and Currency" published in 1936, Keynes assumes that the market economy is not capable of regulating itself, thus not guaranteeing low levels of unemployment and high levels of production in the long run, being subject to large fluctuations, which would be due to changes in the general level of private investments. For Keynes, contrary to what neoclassical economists assumed, the Great Depression could not be eliminated quickly by natural market forces, since some basic prices of the economy, such as wages, are not flexible enough to adjust economic shocks. Keynes proposed expanding government spending and changing monetary and fiscal policies to address the problems of the Great Depression. He advocated the use of stabilization policies to regulate the economy. According to classical theory, the labor market would naturally adjust to ensure full employment in the long run. The Great Depression would eventually demonstrate the fallacy of the classical hypothesis and, in particular, Say's famous Law.

## 4.5. The Keynesian Revolution

John Maynard Keynes is the creator of modern macroeconomics, and his works broke with the neoclassical tradition by presenting a program of government action to promote full employment. Keynes was interested in the problems of short-term economic instability and sought to determine the causes of economic fluctuations and the levels of income and employment in industrial economies. Keynes, intellectually trained according to neoclassical principles, questioned those principles, including his long-term concerns, "a period in which we will all be dead", according to Keynes.

Keynes analyzed the problems of large aggregates in the short term (income, employment, savings, consumption, investment) and contested the Marxist critique of capitalism which, for Keynes, could be preserved, in its essential part, if appropriate reforms were implemented. Keynes criticized Say's Law and his notion of perpetual balance between supply and demand: for him the big problem in the post-Great Depression period was an insufficient effective demand (consumption plus investment) that kept the American economy in depression. Keynes analyzed the problem of currency retention ("liquidity trap") and analyzed the large aggregates of the economy and the balance of these aggregates, assigning an active role to fiscal policy - the political use of public deficits - and giving little importance to monetary policy.

Keynes, unlike Adam Smith and the other classical economists, sought to recover the mercantilist legacy, emphasizing the importance of surpluses in the trade balance in reducing interest rates and increasing effective demand. The principle of effective demand, perfected by Keynes, is not new in economic theory. Thomas Malthus (1766-1790) and John Hobson (1858-1940) had already made a similar argument. Furthermore, Joan Robinson (1903-1983), in his work 'Freedom and Necessity', shows that the main theses of the General Theory had already been anticipated by Gunnar Myrdal (1898-1987) and Michael Kalecki (1899-1970), with the ignorance of Keynes.

According to Keynes, a capitalist economy can achieve its equilibrium, even if there is no full use of productive resources. In the Keynesian conception, an economic policy that seeks full employment should:

- **Lower the interest rate.**
- **Increase public spending.**
- **Expand the volume of government loans.**

Keynes rejects Say's Law, which presupposed a perpetual balance between supply and demand, introducing the hypothesis of insufficient demand as the fundamental economic problem in the circumstances of the Great Depression. The concept of effective demand has investment as its main determinant. The spending decisions of economic agents, in the short term, determine the volumes of investment, income and employment. Therefore, actual demand may be less than supply, causing a reduction in production and employment. The currency is also considered as a store of value, with the possibility of hoarding by the economic agents, discouraging demand. Thus, Keynes introduces the concept of liquidity preference and admits demand for money with an end (reasons for precaution and speculation). It also assumes the possibility of a balance with unemployment in the short term, which for the classics and neoclassic would be unacceptable.

Keynes' main economic ideas, in general, therefore, are:

• The level of employment depends on the effective demand, that is, on spending on consumption and investment.

• In a monetary economy (where there is no barter), Say's Law is not valid, given that the perceived income may not be fully consumed.

• In a capitalist economy, there may be advantages in retaining money, if there is a preference for liquidity according to economic expectations. In this case, total sales may exceed total purchases, forcing inventory build-up and overproduction, leading to a drop in sales. If money is hoarded because of a preference for liquidity, effective demand falls.

• The level of consumption depends on income, but it is more stable than the same. When income increases, there is an increase in savings.

• Entrepreneurs will only invest in their businesses if the interest rate is lower than the profit perspective, which Keynes called "marginal efficiency of capital". For investment to occur, the market interest rate must be lower than the marginal efficiency of capital; that is, the expectation of profits in economic activity. If interest rates rise, effective demand falls and vice versa.

• A capitalist economy can find its equilibrium level (savings equal to investment) without the full use of the factors of production.

• To have full employment, it is necessary to use policies that induce the growth of effective demand. For that, the State must be interventionist, fixing low interest rates and increasing public spending and loans to the private sector.

The period of peak Keynesian thought, focusing attention on the demand side, to the detriment of the supply side, goes from 1936 until the early 1970's, when the developed capitalist economies faced problems of inflation and economic stagnation caused largely by the 1973 and 1979 oil shocks. From that period onwards, there was a rise in neoliberal ideas and a retraction in interventionist ideas, in which the role of the State in the economy is increasingly questioned, at a time when the recession caused significant increases in the public deficit and public debt in developed economies. The deepening of the so-called "globalization" appears amid this theoretical paradigm shift from the 1970's.

The "Golden Age of Capitalism" - period 1945-1973 - was of great economic prosperity for the main capitalist nations. There are several factors that eventually contributed to this prosperity:

• The use of Keynesian macroeconomic policies, stimulating aggregate demand and reducing short-term economic fluctuations.

• The adoption of public policies to support the unemployed, the elderly, the sick, etc., which characterize the Social Welfare State, generating access to income for an important portion of the needy population, notably in Western Europe.

• The reconstruction of the European (Marshall Plan) and Japanese economies in the post-World War II period.

• The creation of a set of Bretton Woods institutions (World Bank System and International Monetary Fund), allowing the increase of international trade through the adoption of fixed exchange rates. The World Bank, created in 1944, resulted from the Bretton

Woods agreement and has had, as one of its main characteristics, the function of offering long-term capital, particularly in the financing of economic development projects (infrastructure, education, health, sanitation, environment, etc.).

• The creation of multilateral organizations to resolve conflicts in international trade, avoiding retaliatory trade defense policies that could hinder this trade (GATT - General Agreement on Trade and Technology, which would become the WTO - World Trade Organization).

• The successive technological developments, allowing the development of mass consumer goods and electronic products, factors that characterized the "consumer society" of that period.

• The return of compulsory loans contracted by the US government to finance the war effort during World War II, causing a wealth effect on the population and strongly stimulating effective demand.

• The intense industrialization process of the so-called peripheral economies of Latin America and Asia, with the consequent demand for inputs, raw materials, machinery and equipment, produced in advanced capitalist countries, notably in the United States.

The Keynesian Revolution gave rise to a whole set of models of economic growth and cyclical fluctuation centered on the interaction between two mechanisms: the multiplier and the accelerator. The first describes the effect of autonomous investment on the expansion of aggregate demand; the second, the effect induced by the expansion of aggregate demand on the propensity to invest.

# 4.6. An "Interview" With John Maynard Keynes

Q - Professor Keynes, you called the theory developed in your main work "General Theory". Why is it called "General"?

A - "I intend to highlight the word "general" to emphasize the contrast between my arguments and conclusions and those of the classical theory in which I graduated, and which governs economic thought, both practical and theoretical, from academic and leaders of this generation, as it has dominated them over the past hundred years."

Q - And what is your objective with this?

A - "I will demonstrate that the postulates of classical theory apply only to a special case and not to the general case, since the situation that it supposes is at the limit of the possible equilibrium situations. Furthermore, the characteristics of this special case are not those of the economic society in which we really live, so that the teachings of that theory would be illusory and harmful if we tried to apply its conclusions to the facts of the experience."

Q - Professor Keynes, according to the precepts of classical economic theory, economic liberalism allows capitalist economies to live, except for short-term adjustments, in a balanced situation. Do you agree with this view?

A - "In my opinion, the celebrated optimism of traditional economic theory, which is what causes economists to be looked at as Candids, who, having retired from the world to cultivate their gardens, claim that everything goes in the best way in the best of possible worlds, as long as we let things go by themselves, stems from the fact that the hindrance that an insufficient effective demand can mean for prosperity has not been taken into account. In a society functioning according to classical postulates, there should be a natural tendency for the optimal use of productive resources. It may well be that classical theory represents the path that our economy should follow. But to suppose that it behaves like this is to suppose all the difficulties resolved."

Q - Professor Keynes, You spoke of effective demand. Could you define it for us?

A - "Effective demand is simply the global income (or product) that entrepreneurs expect to receive, including rents that they pass on to other production factors through the volume of employment they decide to grant. The global demand function relates several hypothetical quantities of employment to the income expected to be obtained from the corresponding production volume; and the effective demand for the global demand function value that becomes reality because, considering the conditions of supply, it corresponds to the level of employment that elevates the entrepreneur's profit prospects to the maximum."

Q - Professor Keynes, You have stated that the final objective of your analysis is to find out what determines the volume of employment. In this sense, you develop the concept of marginal propensity to consume, which in your view has important effects on the level of global demand and, therefore, on the level of employment. What is the marginal propensity to consume and what is its relationship with the multiplier principle?

A - "In certain circumstances, it is possible to establish a defined relationship, which we will call Multiplier, between income and investment, and, subject to some simplifications, between total employment and employment directly linked to investment (which we call primary employment). This new step is an integral part of our theory of employment, since, given the propensity to consume, it establishes a precise relationship between the flow of investment and the global volumes of employment and income (....). However, before reaching the multiplier, it is important to introduce the concept of marginal propensity to consume (...). Our normal psychological law that, in the case of variations in the real income of the community, consumption varies, but not so fast, can therefore be translated (...) by the proposition that the variation in consumption and the variation in income have the same sign, but the variation in income is greater than the variation in consumption. Therefore, we define the variation in consumption given a variation in income as the marginal propensity to consume. This quantity is of considerable importance, as it tells us how the next increase in production will be divided between consumption and investment. Because the variation in income is equal to the variation in consumption plus the variation in investment, we can write that the variation in income is equal to a constant (k) time the variation in investment. We call k the investment multiplier. It tells us that when there is an increase in total investment, the rent rises by an amount equal to k times the increase in investment."

Q - Professor Keynes, You have defended government spending as a way of bringing economies to full employment, because, in your view, these expenditures have a multiplier effect on aggregate demand and thus on the level of employment. How is this possible?

A - "When the community's psychological attitude towards consumption encourages, for example, to consume nine tenths of an increase in income, the k multiplier is equal to 10, and the total employment caused (for example) by an increase in public expenditure will be ten times higher than the primary employment provided by them, assuming there is no reduction in investment in other sectors."

Q - But Professor Keynes, does not the search for full employment with increased government spending cause inflation?

A - "When full employment is achieved, if investment is sought to increase further, prices tend to rise without limit, whatever the marginal propensity to consume, that is, a state of true inflation is reached. So far, however, rising prices will go hand in hand with an increase in global income."

Q - In your analysis, Professor Keynes, of the determinants of investment, you attach great importance to the marginal efficiency of capital and to the interest rate, which, in your view, is the reward of renouncing liquidity. What is the marginal efficiency of capital?

A - "The relationship between the probable income of a good and its offer price or replacement cost, that is, the relationship between the probable income and the production cost of a supplementary unit of that capital, gives us the marginal efficiency of capital of that type. More precisely, we will define the marginal efficiency of capital as the discount rate that, applied to the series of annuities constituted by the probable income of that capital throughout its existence, would make the present value of these annuities equal to the offer price of the capital. This gives us the marginal efficiencies of different types of capital. The highest of these marginal efficiencies can be considered as the marginal efficiency of capital in general (...). It has since become apparent that the real current investment rate tends to increase until there is no longer a category of capital whose marginal efficiency exceeds the current interest rate. In other words, the investment rate will move to the point of the investment demand scale where the marginal efficiency of capital is generally equal to the market interest rate."

Q - Professor Keynes, academic and business circles have emphasized that the rise in interest rates is leading the country to discourage investment and, therefore, to the economic crisis. What do you think about it?

A - "Now, in our explanations of the phenomenon of the "crisis", we have become accustomed to insisting on the fact that the interest rate tends to rise under the effect of a greater demand for money, both for the purposes of transactions and for speculative. Undoubtedly, sometimes this factor can certainly play a role in aggravating and perhaps, occasionally, triggering. But I believe that the most normal and sometimes essential explanation of the crisis is not primarily a rise in interest rates, but a sudden collapse in the marginal efficiency of capital (...). Pessimism and uncertainty about the future that accompany a collapse in the marginal efficiency of capital, lead to a sharp increase in the preference for liquidity - and therefore a rise in interest rates. The fact that the drop in marginal efficiency of capital is often accompanied by a rise in interest rates, can make the decline in investment much more serious. But the essence of such a state of affairs, however, lies in the drop in the marginal efficiency of capital, especially in the case of the categories of capital that, in the course of the previous phase, most participated in the large new investments."

Q - Professor Keynes, why is combating inflation, in addition to being an objective of economic policy, also an objective of a social nature?

A - "Lenin, it is said, declared that the best way to destroy the capitalist system is to demoralize the currency. Through an ongoing process of inflation, governments can secretly and unknowingly confiscate an important part of their citizens' wealth. With this method, they not only confiscate, but they confiscate arbitrarily; and, while the process impoverishes many, in fact it enriches some."

Q – So, Professor Keynes, can the existence of high inflation generate social and political upheavals?

A - "Those to whom the system brings extraordinary gains, in addition to their merits and even beyond their expectations and desires, become "speculators", objects of hatred by the bourgeoisie - impoverished by inflationism - as well as by the hatred of the proletariat."

Q – So, Professor Keynes, Lenin was right with your proposition?

A - "Evidently Lenin was correct. There is no more subtle or safer way to upset the base of society than to corrupt the currency. The process immobilizes all hidden forces of economic law to destruction."

Q - But, Professor Keynes, how do governments manage to confiscate the wealth of citizens in an unnoticed and secret way?

A - "(...) the governments (...) many of whom are now as imprudent in their methods as they are weak, try to divert the popular indignation against the most obvious consequences of their methods to the so-called "speculators" class."

Q - Could you tell us who these "speculators" are?

A - "These "speculators" speaking in a broad sense, are the entrepreneurial class of capitalists, that is, the active and constructive element of the whole of capitalist society, which, in a period of rapidly rising prices, cannot help enriching, like it or not."

Q - How does this happen, Professor Keynes?

A - "If prices rise continuously, any trader who has formed stocks or who owns or manufactures inevitably makes a profit."

Q - And what are the consequences of this process?

A - "By directing hatred against this class, therefore, governments ... are taking the fatal process that Lenin's subtle mind consciously conceived of one step further. The profiteers are a consequence and not a cause of the rising prices. Combining popular hatred of the business class with the blow to social security already caused by the violent and arbitrary disturbance of the contract and the established balance of wealth - which inevitably results from inflation - these governments are quickly making it impossible for the economic and social order to continue. (...). "

Q - Professor Keynes, could you explain better the social consequences of inflation?

A - "(...) a variation in the value of money, that is, in the price level, is only important for society to the extent that its incidence is unequal (...). As we know, when the currency value changes, it does not change equally for all people and for all purposes. Thus, a change in prices and earnings, measured in cash, generally affects different classes unequally, transfers wealth from one to another, produces opulence here and there the need, redistributes fortune favors in such a way that design and hope is disappointed."

Q - But, if this occurs, what determines its existence?

A - "This progressive deterioration of the currency's value, throughout history, is not an accident, with two major driving forces behind it - the impeccability of governments and the superior political influence of the debtor class."

Q - Does this mean that it has always existed?

A - "The power of taxation for currency depreciation has been inherent in the state since Rome discovered it."

Q - Could you explain it better?

A - "The creation of money has been and is a final resource of the government, and it is not likely that a state or government will decree its own bankruptcy or its own fall until it has used this instrument. (...) To some extent, under the influence of governments and the political influence of the debtor class, sometimes from one and sometimes from another, the progress of inflation has been continuous, if we consider long periods, since the money was conceived in century VI b. C."

Q - "Professor Keynes, could you explain how inflation transfers income to capitalists?

A - "When the value of the currency decreases, it is evident that people committed to the payment of fixed annual sums, based on the profits of active businesses, should benefit, provided that their fixed monetary expenses represent a decreasing proportion of their turnover of money (...). Then, when prices are rising, the borrower becomes able to pay the lender with something that, in terms of real value, not only does not represent any interest but, in addition, is even lower than the capital originally advanced."

**Q** - Could you explain to us better why this is not good for capitalism?

**A** - "The exceptional profits of the businessman appear to the consumer as the cause (and not the consequence) of the hated price increase. Amid the rapid fluctuation of his fortunes, the entrepreneur himself loses his instinct for conservation, starting to think more about the big gains of the moment than the smaller, but permanent, profits of normal businesses. His company's prosperity in the relatively distant future weighs less than before, and his thoughts are excited by his quick fortune and eagerness to sell (...). In his heart, he loses his old self-confidence in relation to society, to his own utility and to the need in the economic scheme (...). The businessman, propellant of society and builder of the future, whose activities and rewards had not long been attributed an almost religious sanction, he - the most respectable among all men and all classes, praiseworthy and necessary, on which interference it was not only necessary but still almost merciless - he should now receive oblique looks, feel suspicious and attacked, victim of unjust and imperious laws to become and thus recognize himself as guilty, a profiteer."

**Q** - And what is the consequence of that?

**A** - "No man of spirit will consent to remain poor, if he believes that his bosses have conquered his assets by playing with his fortune. To convert the entrepreneur into a speculator is to strike capitalism, because it destroys the psychological balance that allows the perpetuation of unequal rewards (...). The entrepreneur is only tolerable as long as it is possible to accept that his earnings are related to what, grossly in any sense, his activities brought as a contribution to society."

Q - Professor Keynes, what do you think about the credit restriction policy to fight inflation?

A - "When investment moves ahead of savings, we have a big increase in activity, intense employment and a tendency to inflation. When investment falls behind, activity falls sharply and abnormal unemployment appears, as now. It is commonly objected that a credit expansion necessarily means inflation. But not all credit creation means inflation. This results only when we try, as in war and soon after, to continue expanding activities after everyone is employed and our savings are being used up. The suggestion that a capital spending policy, if it does not divert capital from common industry, will mean inflation, would be quite true if we were faced with conditions of high activity (...). To evoke the inflation demon as an objection to capital expenditure, in these times, is like warning of the dangers of excessive corpulence to a patient who is dying out of thinness."

Q - Professor Keynes, one of the causes pointed out as having a negative effect on the economy is the high interest rate. How can this problem be solved?

A - "The interest rate can fall for one or another of two opposite reasons. It may fall because of an abundant supply of savings, that is, money available to be spent on investments; or it may fall because of a deficient supply of investments, that is, desirable objectives on which to spend savings. Now, a fall in interest rates for the first reason is obviously much more suited to national interest. A fall for the second reason, however, if it follows a deliberate restriction of investment opportunities, is simply a disastrous method of impoverishing us."

Q - What do you mean, Mr. Keynes?

A - "A country is enriched not by the simple negative act of individuals not spending all their income on current consumption. It is enriched by the positive act of using these savings to increase the country's capital stock. (...) The objective of encouraging people to save is designed to create the capacity to build houses, roads and so on. Therefore, a policy aimed at trying to reduce the interest rate by suspending further additions to the capital stock (...) is simply suicidal."

Q - You have criticized the government's economic policy. But are the results in terms of foreign trade not favorable?

A - "The futility of your policy and the lack of sound thinking behind it was demonstrated, finally, by the failure to even guarantee a drop in interest rates. Because (...) if domestic investment opportunities cease, savings go abroad on a scale disproportionate to our favorable trade balance."

Q - Do you mean that the economic situation is really difficult?

A - "In the end, therefore, we have the worst of worlds. The country is lagging behind in terms of equipment, rather than being entirely up to date. Corporate profits are poor, with the result that their income tax receipts disappoint the Treasury Minister, who is unable both to relieve the taxpayer and to carry out social reform schemes. Unemployment is violent. This lack of prosperity effectively lowers the savings rate and thus overturns even the original goal of a low interest rate. So, the rates are, after all, high."

Q - Do you attribute this situation to the government's conservative economic policy?

A - "It is not an accident that the Conservative Government has thrown us into the mess we are in. It is the natural result of his philosophy:

"You shouldn't press for phone or electricity because that would raise the interest rate."

"Road and housing works should not be accelerated, as this would deplete job opportunities that we may need in future years."

"One should not try to employ everyone, as this will cause inflation."

"We will not promise more than we can achieve. Soon, we will not promise anything."

# 4.7. Author's Notes

### 4.7.1. The Paris Peace Conference

The Paris Peace Conference began on January 18, 1919 and ended on January 20, 1920, with the presence of 70 delegates from the 27 countries victorious in World War I and resulted in the Treaty of Versailles signed on June 28 of 1919, which defined the terms in which peace with defeated nations would be promoted: to establish a new political map of Europe, the war indemnities and the demilitarization conditions of the vanquished countries, in order to reduce the size of their military forces .

Brazil was represented by a delegation headed by the future president Epitácio Pessoa and managed to include in the peace agreement the compensation for coffee bags seized in German ports during the war and the sale of German ships taken during the war.

### 4.7.2. The 1919 Treaty of Versailles

The 1919 Treaty of Versailles was a peace treaty signed by the European powers that officially ended the First World War and determined that Germany should assume all responsibilities for provoking the war and that it should make reparations to some nations of the Triple Entente.

The conditions imposed on Germany - extremely harsh - included the loss of part of its territory in favor of some neighboring nations, of all colonies over the oceans and in Africa, a decrease in the size of its army and compensation for the damages caused by the war, in addition to the recognition of Austria's independence. The treaty was ratified by the League of Nations on January 10, 1920. In Germany, the treaty provoked deep popular indignation, which certainly contributed to the fall of the regime in 1933, the rise of Hitler and Nazism and the beginning of the Second World War. Other clauses included the loss of German colonies and territories that the country had annexed or invaded.

### 4.7.3. The Bretton Woods Conferences

The Bretton Woods Conferences took place in Bretton Woods, New Hampshire, United States, in July 1944, therefore, one year before the end of World War II, defining what was conventionally called the Bretton Woods System of international economic administration, which set the rules for commercial and financial relations between the most industrialized countries in the world. Such a system was the first successful example in world history of a fully negotiated monetary order, with the aim of managing monetary and financial relations between nations. The Bretton Woods agreement resulted in the creation of the World Bank and the International Monetary Fund.

### 4.7.4. The World Bank

The World Bank was formally created on December 27, 1945, following what was established the previous year in the Bretton Woods Agreement by 44 countries. The World Bank is currently headquartered in Washington and consists of 184 member countries.

The World Bank is an agency that is part of the United Nations System and consists of a group of 5 (five) institutions that includes IBRD - International Bank for Reconstruction and Development, AID - International Development Association, IFC - International Finance Corporation, AMGI - Multilateral Investment Guarantee Agency and CIADI - International Center for Investment Dispute Arbitration.

### 4.7.5. The IMF - International Monetary Fund

The IMF - International Monetary Fund, created on December 27, 1945, together with the World Bank, following the provisions of the Bretton Woods Agreement, in 1944, is headquartered in Washington, United States, and is currently constituted by 185 countries. Ideologically, the IMF defends the free market and the elimination of exchange rate barriers.

The primary objective of the IMF is to seek stability in the international monetary-financial system, promoting balance in the balance of payments and in international exchange systems and, thus, favoring the sustained expansion of trade and global financial flows. However, the IMF currently seeks to expand its objectives, including combating global poverty as one of its goals.

The IMF also sponsors structural adjustment and balance of payments programs, as well as providing technical assistance and training in various areas to different member countries.

Traditionally, the World Bank is chaired by an American, in the same way that the IMF is chaired by a European.

## 4.7.6. Say's Law

According to Say's Law, "supply creates its own demand" (expression coined by John Maynard Keynes). People offer a good or service to acquire other goods. By this mechanism, it would not be possible to have overproduction in the free-market capitalist economy, that is, there would be no mismatch between supply and demand because payments to factors of production (wages, profits, interest) that constitute production costs correspond to the flow of money. income needed to purchase the goods. The Great Depression (1929) buried Say's Law. There was widespread overproduction in the world capitalist system (mainly in the United States) and it opened space for the emergence of the Keynesian Revolution.

Jean-Baptiste Say (1768-1830)

Say's Law is presented in the following passage of his work:

"It is worthwhile to remark that a product is no sooner created than it, from that instant, affords a market for other products to the full extent of its own value. When the producer has put the finishing hand to his product, he is most anxious to sell it immediately, lest its value should diminish in his hands. Nor is he less anxious to dispose of the money he may get for it; for the value of money is also perishable. But the only way of getting rid of money is in the purchase of some product or other. Thus, the mere circumstance of creation of one product immediately opens a vent for other products." (Jean-Baptiste Say, A Treatise on Political Economy, 1803: pp.138–139).

David Ricardo accepted Say's Law, but Thomas Malthus rejected it completely, with the argument that effective demand tends to be less than supply, because, in Malthus's view, the capitalist class has a tendency not to spend its income, preferring to treasure a significant portion of the profits it receives. Keynes also criticized Say's Law, with arguments similar to those used by Malthus, that the increase in savings could reduce the rate of profit, leading to hoarding and, consequently, to the reduction of effective demand.

# 5. AN "INTERVIEW" WITH MILTON FRIEDMAN (1912-2006)

"The preservation of freedom is the main reason for the limitation and decentralization of government power. But there is also a constructive reason. The great advances of civilization - whether in architecture or painting, in science or literature, in industry or agriculture - never came from centralized governments."

Milton Friedman
(1912-2006)

**Milton Friedman**

# 5.1. Who Was Milton Friedman

Milton Friedman, an American economist, was born on July 31, 1912, in Brooklyn, New York, and died on November 16, 2006. Son of Russian immigrant parents and a poor family, he was awarded a scholarship at the age of 16 for the University of Rutgers, in New Brunswick, after finishing the basic cycle, coming to finish his studies in 1932.

Friedman's academic career begins to take shape and direction when he chooses the University of Chicago to pursue a master's degree in economics, completing it in 1933.

The Department of Economics of that University, under the leadership of Frank Knight (1885-1972), defended economic liberalism and decentralization, therefore, non-state intervention as an ideal way to provide maximum welfare to society, that is, a maximum competitiveness system.

After a stint at Columbia University, where he is influenced by the "institutionalists" and for his participation in the New Deal Program in Washington, in the period 1935-37, Friedman, at the invitation of Simon Kuznets (1901-1985), goes to work in National Office of Economic Research, in New York, where he develops a work related to the evaluation of income of liberal professionals in the United States, which came to become his PhD thesis, which suffered a series of restrictions, for reasons that are not very clear, from questions related to writing, to criticisms about some conclusions. This thesis, completed in 1941, was only approved in 1946.

In the 1940-41 period, Friedman teaches at the University of Wisconsin, as a visiting professor, and then returns to the University of Columbia, following an invitation to do a study on the forecast and control of inflation.

After short visits to the Treasury, the University of Columbia and the University of Minnesota, Friedman joined the University of Chicago in 1946, where he began to develop in-depth studies on the role of liberalism as a philosophy of social organization and where he remained until he ended his career.

Milton Friedman served as economic advisor to three US presidents, Richard Nixon (1913-1994), Gerald Ford (1913-2006) and Ronald Reagan (1911-2004) and published several books on macroeconomics, microeconomics, monetary theory, statistics and economic history.

An aspect considered by many less noble in his biography is its relationship with Augusto Pinochet's regime (1915-2006) in Chile, as his liberal economic ideas strongly influenced that country's economic policy throughout the 1970s, and Friedman did not criticize the lack of political freedom of the then Chilean dictatorial regime.

The evolution of Friedman's thinking moves towards giving a prominent role to monetary policy - in contrast to Keynesian ideas, which are more relevant to fiscal policy - and to liberalism. This line of thought took its definitive form in the early 1960s, with the publication of "Capitalism and Freedom" (1962) and "Monetary History of the United States" (1963), the second with the collaboration of Anna Schwartz (1915-2012), works that will frame his "monetarist theory". According to the authors, economic fluctuations were the result of changes in the money supply, prescribing a stable and constant money supply to achieve lasting economic stability.

Friedman's line of thought represents the resumption of liberal ideas by classical economists in the 18th century and marginalists in the 19th century, linked to an important role reserved for monetary policy and opposition to discretionary policies (monetary or fiscal) as a way of resolving problems of depression or recession, because they, in Friedman's view, concerned with short-term solutions, lose their long-term vision and, therefore, become ineffective. Friedman tried to show that the State, contrary to what many imagine, can turn against the interests of the citizens, insofar as the bigger it is, the greater greed for resources it will have and, therefore, the greater the transfer of resources from society to it, with dubious application from the point of view of efficient resource allocation, and the greater the restrictions on citizens' freedom.

For Friedman, inflation is fundamentally a monetary problem and, therefore, for inflation there must also be an increase in the stock of money. Friedman criticizes the Keynesians for attaching importance to non-monetary factors in explaining inflation. For him, non-monetary factors can, in certain circumstances, cause inflation, if they cause monetary expansion. According to Friedman, it is generally said that there are three ways in which the government can obtain funds: tax, borrowing from the population or print money. For him this is a mistake, as there are only two means: taxes and loans, since the printing of money is either a loan or is imposed. For Friedman, there is a logical incompatibility between Socialism and Democracy: a socialist society cannot also be democratic in the sense of guaranteeing individual freedom.

According to Friedman, the liberal is not an anarchist and, therefore, he is not against the action of the state. Thus, he accepts a government that maintains law and order; define property rights; serve as a means of modifying property rights and other rules of the economic game; judge disputes over the interpretation of the rules; enforce contracts; promote competition; provide a monetary structure; engage in activities to avoid technical monopoly; and, finally, supplement private charity and the family in protecting the irresponsible.

The consistency of his stance and the results of his research gave him, in 1976, the Nobel Prize in Economics, and made Friedman an economist who is already part of the history of economic thought, for his valuable contribution to Economics as Science and to preservation of freedom as a principle, means and end.

## 5.2. An "Interview" with Milton Friedman

Q - Professor Friedman, do you think that inflation is an inevitable consequence of the search for economic growth by developing countries?

A - "It is widely known that inflation is inevitable in a country that wants to force its pace of development. In general, the argument follows the following lines: when a country tries to accelerate the pace of its development, it exerts strong pressure on the available resources. Consequently, there is an increase in demand, which can only be met by rising prices. It is then said that the development process is certainly driving up prices. Such an argument, however, confuses physical quantities with monetary quantities. Pressure on resources during the development process affects relative prices. It tends to increase, compared to other articles, the price of those whose demand is higher, in the development process. However, it does not need to affect the absolute price level. It all depends on how the real resources needed for development are obtained. If, for example, these real resources are obtained, by the government, through taxes or public loans, or by private companies and individuals, with their own investment savings, there will be no pressure from the monetary demand. There will be a shift in demand for certain products to others, thus motivating the necessary shift of real resources. On the other hand, if we use the printing press or any of its modern and sophisticated substitutes, to acquire resources, there will be a tendency for inflation and price increases."

Q - Professor Friedman, what are the causes of inflation and what is the difference between your way of explaining the causes of inflation and the others? What is the fundamental difference?

A - "(...) I would like to elaborate a little further by analyzing the causes of inflation, since it is considered out of fashion and the emphasis with which, until now, I have attributed the responsibility for inflation to the monetary stock has been overcome. Most modern authors attribute it to quite different causes. They say that it is the result of an imbalance between the investments that were tried and the savings that the population would be inclined to make; wage pressure on the part of employees; pressure from employers and entrepreneurs to increase their profits; the inability to get the increase in food production to keep pace with the production of other articles; and so on, with several and different causes being pointed out. Now, all of these explanations may, in a way, be correct. If any of these factors contribute to the increase in the money stock, it will give rise to inflation, but if it does not lead to an increase in the money stock, it will not produce inflation."

Q - Professor Friedman, why, in your opinion, do these theories that you criticize have great acceptability in Academy?

A - "It is not difficult to find reasons for the great popularity of these theories. There are two, I believe. The first is the natural tendency to confuse what is true for the individual with what is true for society. The most important and interesting fact about the economic sciences is exactly that almost every rule that applies to individuals is not valid for society and almost everything that is valid for society is not valid for the individual. An individual can hardly, in general, influence the price of what he buys. However, all individuals, together, make price what it is. In the case of inflation, for each individual individually, the increase in prices is in no way related to the fact that these pieces of paper that we all like to have in our pockets have been scattered around the printer. The entrepreneur raises his prices because, on the one hand, the costs have gone up and on the other, he feels that he can get an even higher price for his product. Thus, for each of us separately, a price increase comes from the increase in any other commodity. We never face the fact that the price rise is ultimately the consequence of the change in more money. The second reason, as important as the first, is that, in modern times, the Government has almost a monopoly on money issuance. This notion is exaggerated (...) because private banks have possibilities to create money, although, in modern countries (...) it can be said, in general, that the Government can control the amount of money, if want to do it."

Q - Professor Friedman, Mr. Keynes had said that governments try to divert popular indignation against inflation into the so-called "speculators" class. Do you agree?

A - "Nobody likes to take the blame for the bad things that happen. Although many people like inflation because it is personally favorable to them, on the other hand, almost everyone considers it an evil and nobody likes to admit that they are responsible for it. For the Government, it is easier to attribute inflation to profiteers, to misguided unions that insist on raising wages or to the misunderstanding of farmers unable to increase food production, than to say mea culpa."

**Q** - Professor Friedman, what is your opinion about Keynesian thinking when it comes to interpreting inflation?

**A** - "(...) the Keynesian revolution of economic thought, which occurred in the 1930s, led many economists to diminish the importance attributed to money. The importance attached to this non-monetarist theory is not new, which is why I consider it to be baseless. We can go back a century or two, even more, and see that, each time inflation occurs, there are two theories to explain it. One refers to the increase in money stock, the other to some special events: increase in wages, great activity by profiteers, blockade of the country, with the consequent impediment of the entry of goods and so on. As I have already noted, these two different explanations are not necessarily contradictory. Non-monetary factors can, in certain circumstances, be the cause of monetary expansion. For example, when someone argues that inflation is because the desired investments are greater than the planned savings, they may be correctly describing a secondary stage in the inflationary process. If the investment attempt was made by the Government and the Government intended to finance the investment by issuing money, then it is certain that the desire to make greater investments than the public's willingness to save causes inflation. It is the cause of inflation because it produces an increase in the money stock. It really happens that in some countries (...) unions can force wages to rise to the point of causing unemployment. If the Government follows a policy of full employment, it can, therefore, expand the money stock, issuing more money to cover public expenditure, or for other purposes (...) The historical evidence is clear: the sources of monetary expansion have been very diverse, in different times and places. Therefore, if an inflation theory does not consider the expansion of the money stock, but the causes of this expansion, it will be a pluralistic theory that will point out many possible causes of inflation (...) I know of no exception to the statement that there is one-to-one relationship between substantial price increases and substantial increases in the money stock. On several occasions I have challenged my interlocutors to cite an exception to me."

**Q** - Professor Friedman, You have emphasized the importance of money in determining prices. Could you explain this relationship a little more?

**A** - "The key to the answer lies in the difference between the nominal amount of money, the amount of money expressed in rupees, dollars, marks, or whatever the currency of a country, and the real amount of money, the amount of money expressed in terms of goods and services, that he can buy or by the number of weeks of income he is equal to. People tend to be extraordinarily obstinate about the actual amount of money they wish to have in their possession and unwilling to accept a different amount, unless they have a real incentive to do so. This is true not only in time but also in space (...) suppose that, for whatever reason, the amount of money in a community exceeds what people want to bring with them, regarding the current price level. For the purpose that we have in mind, we do not care why, either because the Government issued to finance the expenses, because someone discovered a gold mine, or because the banks found a way to create deposits (...) What will be the result? Here too, it is essential to distinguish what will happen to the individual and the community. Everyone, separately, thinks he can get rid of money, and he is right. You can go out and spend it, thereby reducing your cash balance. But for the community the belief that the monetary balance can be reduced is just an optical illusion. The only reason I can decrease my balance in nominal terms is that someone is increasing yours. One man's spending corresponds to another man's income. The population cannot spend more than they receive (...) In the process of trying to spend more than they earn, people raise the prices of all sorts of goods and services."

**Q** - Professor Friedman, what do you think about the commonly held thesis that inflation stimulates economic development?

A - "There are two main arguments that have been used to support the thesis that inflation stimulates economic development. The first is that inflation tends to redistribute income and wealth. They say that inflation redistributes money, taking it away from the wage classes, whose tendency is to consume it entirely, for the benefit of those living on a profit in the community and who, in addition to saving a lot, invest their savings in productive capital. It is further argued that inflation redistributes capital, taking it from the hands of creditors, people who lend money, but are considered unproductive, and passing it on to those of borrowers, people who borrow money, supposedly for productive purposes. The second argument (...) is the statement that the issue of money is a source of income for the Government and, as such, provides it with funds that can be used to promote development (...) redistribution of income and wealth, there is no doubt that, in certain circumstances, in the past, this redistribution was favorable to development (...) The discoveries of gold and silver in the New World produced an influx of coins, initially in Spain , which have spread across Europe and the world. (....) the price increase originating from this influx of cash has strongly stimulated development (...) The reason for stopping inflation causing such an effect (...) is that it was unexpected. The result is that the population clung to traditional levels of prices and interest, with the consequent transfer of income from wage earners in favor of those who live on profits and the transfer of capital from creditors to debtors (...) I am extremely skeptical when it comes to affirming that it is possible to obtain a similar result through a deliberate process of expanding the money stock, without the thing degenerating into hyperinflation."

Q - Why, Mr. Friedman?


A - "If the decision was deliberate, many people would become aware of it and will act in a way that prevents redistribution."


Q - Professor Friedman, You spoke of the argument that inflation is a way for the Government to raise funds ....

A - "It is generally said that there are three ways in which the Government can obtain funds: tax, borrow from the population or print money. This is a mistake. There are only two means (...): taxes and loans (...) Printing money is either a loan or a tax. To the extent that money can be issued without raising prices, the Government is obtaining resources through loans (....) On the other hand, if the issue of money raises prices, then the Government obtains resources through means of tax."

Q - Professor Friedman, is it possible, in your view, to have coexistence between Socialism and Democracy?

A - "It is generally believed that politics and economics constitute separate territories, presenting very few interrelations; that individual freedom is a political problem and material well-being an economic problem; and that any type of political organization can be combined with any type of economic organization. The most important contemporary manifestation of this idea is reflected in the concept of "democratic socialism", when the restrictions on individual freedom imposed by "totalitarian socialism" in Russia are condemned and it is considered possible to adopt the essential characteristics of the Russian economic organization and, at the same time, to guarantee individual freedom through a certain political organization (...) Such a point of view is purely illusory (...) A socialist society cannot also be democratic in the sense of guaranteeing individual freedom."

Q - Could you explain better this antagonism between Socialism and individual freedom?

A - "Economic organization plays a dual role in promoting a free society. On the one hand, economic freedom is part of freedom understood in the broadest sense and, therefore, an end. Second, economic freedom is also an indispensable instrument for the achievement of political freedom (...) the citizens of Great Britain, who, after the Second World War, were not allowed to vacation in the United States due to control exchange rates, were being deprived of essential freedom. The same was true of citizens of the United States who were denied the right to vacation in the Soviet Union because of their political views. The first was ostensibly an economic limitation of freedom and the second, a political limitation, but there is no essential difference between the two."

Q - For you, then, there is a close relationship between the type of economic organization and political freedom. How does this happen?

A - "Seen to obtain political freedom, economic organization is important due to its effect on the concentration or dispersion of power. The type of economic organization that directly promotes economic freedom, that is, competitive capitalism, also promotes political freedom because it separates economic power from political power and thus allows one to control the other. Historical evidence speaks unanimously of the relationship between political freedom and the free market. I do not know of any example of a society that had great political freedom and that also did not use something comparable to a free market to organize most of the economic activity."

Q - Professor Friedman, how would you rate the types of current economic organizations?

A - "Fundamentally, there are only two ways to coordinate the economic activities of millions. One is the central direction using coercion - the technique of the modern totalitarian army and state. The other is the voluntary cooperation of individuals - the technique of the market."

Q - Professor Friedman, You have been insistently emphasizing the role of the free market in achieving social well-being. Could you explain this role to us?

A - "The role of the market (...) is to allow unanimity without conformity and to be a system of effective proportional representation."

Q - Professor Friedman, You often say that on some issues it is impossible to have effective proportional representation. For example, in terms of the amount of national defense that each citizen wants. Is that where, in your opinion, the State should assume its functions as legislator and arbitrator?

A - "The basic roles of government in a free society are to provide the means to modify the rules, to regulate differences in their meaning, and to ensure compliance with the rules by those who would not otherwise submit to them. The government's need in this area arises because absolute freedom is impossible (...) The freedoms of men can conflict, and when that happens, the freedom of some must be limited to preserve that of others."

Q - Professor Friedman, in addition to these functions, you have mentioned others that the government could assume, if they are limited and under the control of society. Could you tell us what they are?

A - "A government that maintains law and order; define property rights; serve as a means of modifying property rights and other rules of the economic game; judge disputes over the interpretation of the rules; enforce contracts; promote competition; provide a monetary structure; engage in activities to avoid technical monopoly and avoid side effects considered to be important enough to justify government intervention; supplement private charity and the family in protecting the irresponsible, whether it be an insane person or a child; such a government would, of course, have important roles to play. The consistent liberal is not an anarchist."

Q - One of the arguments used by Keynes to justify the intervention of the State in the Economy, was that the capitalist system, contrary to what the classical economists claimed, was unstable. What do you think about it?


A - "Total employment" and "economic growth" have been the main justifications for the expansion of government intervention in economic matters in recent decades. The free enterprise economy, they say, is inherently unstable. Left to its own devices, it would produce cycles of ups and downs. The government must therefore intervene to keep things in balance. These arguments were particularly powerful during and after the Great Depression of 1930 and constituted important elements for the emergence of the New Deal in this country and for comparable extensions of government intervention in other countries. More recently, "economic growth" has become the most important slogan for political meetings. The government must, it is said, guarantee the expansion of the economy in order to obtain resources for the cold war and demonstrate to the non-aligned nations of the world that a democracy can grow faster than the communist state. These arguments are completely wrong. It turns out that the Great Depression, similarly to other periods of great unemployment, was caused by the incompetence of the government - and not by the instability inherent in the private initiative. One government organization - the Federal Reserve System - had responsibility for monetary policy. In 1930 and 1931, he exercised such responsibility so ineptly that he ended up converting what otherwise would have been a moderate contraction into a major catastrophe. Today, similarly, government measures are the biggest impediment to economic growth in the United States. Tariffs and other restrictions on international trade, heavy taxation and a complex and unfair taxation structure, regulatory commissions, government wage and price fixing and a huge number of other measures provide individuals with an incentive for the inconvenient and inappropriate use of resources and distort investment from new savings. In fact, we urgently need, for stability and economic growth, a reduction in government intervention - not expansion."

## 6. Bibliography

The Thinkers Collection, Abril Cultural.
J. M. Keynes, The General Theory of Employment, Interest and Currency, Nova Cultural, 1985.
Simonsen & Cysne, Macroeconomics, 1995.